SECOND EDITION

The Definitive Personal Assistant & Secretarial Handbook

Sue France

KoganPage

LONDON PHILADELPHIA NEW DELHI

Publisher's note

Every possible effort has been made to ensure that the information contained in this book is accurate at the time of going to press, and the publishers and author cannot accept responsibility for any errors or omissions, however caused. No responsibility for loss or damage occasioned to any person acting, or refraining from action, as a result of the material in this publication can be accepted by the editor, the publisher or the author.

First published in Great Britain and the United States in 2009 by Kogan Page Limited
Second edition, 2012

Apart from any fair dealing for the purposes of research or private study, or criticism or review, as permitted under the Copyright, Designs and Patents Act 1988, this publication may only be reproduced, stored or transmitted, in any form or by any means, with the prior permission in writing of the publishers, or in the case of reprographic reproduction in accordance with the terms and licences issued by the CLA. Enquiries concerning reproduction outside these terms should be sent to the publishers at the undermentioned addresses:

120 Pentonville Road	1518 Walnut Street, Suite 1100	4737/23 Ansari Road
London N1 9JN	Philadelphia PA 19102	Daryaganj
United Kingdom	USA	New Delhi 110002
www.koganpage.com		India

ISBN   978 0 7494 6576 6
E-ISBN   978 0 7494 6577 3

British Library Cataloguing-in-Publication Data

A CIP record for this book is available from the British Library.

Library of Congress Cataloging-in-Publication Data

France, Sue.
   The definitive personal assistant & secretarial handbook : a best practice guide for all secretaries, PAs, office managers, and executive assistants / Sue France. – 2nd ed.
      p. cm.
   Includes index.
   ISBN 978-0-7494-6576-6 – ISBN 978-0-7494-6577-3   1. Administrative assistants–Handbooks, manuals, etc.   2. Secretaries–Handbooks, manuals, etc.   3. Office management–Handbooks, manuals, etc.   4. Office practice–Handbooks, manuals, etc.   I. Title.   II. Title: The definitive personal assistant and secretarial handbook.
   HF5547.5.F69 2012
   651–dc23
                                                                                            2012007730

Typeset by Graphicraft Limited, Hong Kong
Printed and bound in India by Replika Press Pvt Ltd

*This new edition is dedicated with all my love to
my two daughters who are beautiful inside and out,
Sara Hoodfar and Samantha Higgins, who continue to
support and encourage me in my work and everything I do.
It is also dedicated to my precious and
wonderful granddaughter, Isabella Rosina Reading,
who always makes me smile and brings even
more joy to my life!*

CONTENTS

ABOUT THE AUTHOR

Sue France started work as a shorthand typist and word-processing operator and worked her way up, becoming a senior secretary, team supervisor, events manager and personal assistant to the head of Andersen in Manchester, a leading global accountancy firm. She attended Salford University as a mature student part time, gaining a post-graduate diploma in human resource management, and became a member and later a fellow of the Chartered Institute of Personnel and Development (CIPD). Sue is a qualified CIPD Learning and Development Practitioner. She then became part of the global training team as training manager responsible for 600 secretaries in the UK and was also responsible for the technology training of all staff. From 2002 to November 2009 Sue worked with Bill Docherty MBE, a former Andersen partner who had left the firm in 2000 to set up his own training and development company – Persuasion.

Sue was Bill's right-hand person working as his personal assistant and events manager. She was also responsible for training and coaching personal/executive assistants and secretaries, and presented at international secretarial conferences on her own as well as with her boss as a boss-and-PA team.

Sue is heavily involved with European Management Assistants (EUMA), a voluntary secretarial networking organization that operates in 25 countries, helping to develop personal/executive assistants and providing global links for the profession. Sue is the UK chairman for EUMA. She was awarded the prestigious title of *The Times* Crème DHL PA of the Year 2006 and was a finalist in the European Smart PA of the Year 2007.

Since May 2010, Sue has been self-employed as a trainer and coach for secretaries, personal assistants, executive assistants and office managers. She has facilitated workshops and presented at conferences worldwide in Sydney, Perth, Melbourne, Brisbane, Johannesburg, Kenya, Zimbabwe, Ireland, Cyprus, France, Germany, Oman, Qatar, Dubai, Bahrain, Kuala Lumpar, Shanghai, Singapore and the UK. Sue strongly believes in continual self-development and has been Certified as a Neuro-Linguistic Programming practitioner and is a certified TetraMap® Facilitator.

How to contact the author: Sue would be delighted to hear from you and is happy to travel anywhere in the world to facilitate workshops and speak at conferences. She is also available for one-to-one coaching in the UK and telephone coaching worldwide. Her e-mail address is **sue@suefrance.com** and she can also be contacted via the website at **www.suefrance.com**.

ACKNOWLEDGEMENTS

I would like to give all my love and thanks for their support to my two wonderful caring and kind daughters: Sara Hoodfar and Samantha Higgins.

A huge thank you to everyone who replied to my questionnaire, especially to those I have quoted in the book, and also to those assistants who wish to remain anonymous. I received replies from secretarial networking organizations and individual personal assistants, executive assistants and secretaries from around the world, including the UK, Germany, Denmark, Poland, Turkey, France, Norway, Iceland, Cyprus, Saudi Arabia, Sweden, South Africa, America, Australia, Switzerland, New Zealand, the United States and more.

I would also like to personally thank:

Legal Secretaries International Inc, USA

European Management Assistants (EUMA)

Australian Institute of Office Professionals (AIOP)

IIR conferences and Office Professionals Australia (OPA)

Association for Office Professionals of South Africa (OPSA)

Association of Administrative Professionals New Zealand Inc (AAPNZ).

and

Mohammed Amin, Rebecca Apel, Barbara Baker, Heather Baker, Susie Baron-Stubley, Tracie Barton, Charlotte Beffert, Brenda Bernstein, Lucy Brazier, Eileen Broadbent, Samantha Brown, Warren Cass, Bianca Constance, Louise Cope, Sarah Crown, Marie Cullis, Francoise Cumming, Julie Daniels, Victoria Darragh, Christine Davies, Bill Docherty MBE, Debs Eden, Narisa B Espinoza, Mary Ferrie, Adam Fidler, Dawn Field, Diane Flynn, Kemetia M K Foley, Mitch France, Jasmine Freeman, Angela Garry, Lisa Gathercole-Smith, Carol Gourlay, Joanna Gutmann, Jade Hall, Laurel Harmen, Dewoun Hayes, Ynske Heeringa, Sarah Hewson, Jill Hodgkinson, Liezel Huyzers, Patricia Jacob, Duda Jadrijevic, Warsha Joshi, Tanya Kay, Debra Kerrigan, Derek Knowles, Jakki Koris, Emma Lambden, Peter Lawrence, Danny Lewis, Sydney Lindeman, Jenni Lumsden, Carmen MacDougall, Aman

Malhotra, Maria McAdam, David McKeith, Fiona McKinnon, David Morel, Nicky Morris, Richard Mullender, Liz O'Farrell, Anne Ormston, *OS Secretarial* magazine, **pa-assist.com**, Paul Pennant, Carmen Perez Pies, Heli Puputti, Wendy Reed, Barbara Rimmer, Carol Ritchie, Siggy Reichstein, Gillian Richmond, Carole Rigney, Anna Ripka, Jeanette Ritzen, Fiona Roberts, Sue Robson, Lisa Rodgers , Beth Ruge, Karen Ryan, Eila Sandberg, Dr Monica Seeley, Luise Seidler, Carole Spiers, Rebecca Stache, Kristy Stewart, Janita C Sullivan, Cheryl Sykes, Melissa Taylor, Shirley Taylor, Brigitte Thethy, Leigh Thomson-Persaud, Nicola Tratalos, Hanne Vinther, Marie Voss, Lesley Watts, David Whitehead, Ben Williams, James Williams, Luke Williams, Amanda Woods and Lea Wray.

Introduction

I have decided to revise this book to make sure it is still relevant for the 21st-century assistant and the evolution of the role. I am also including two new chapters on social media and minute-taking. All assistants in every sector need to understand social media and how they can impact on their lives and their jobs as well as on their bosses' lives and organizations. I have added a full chapter on how to take minutes in detail to enable you to take part in your meetings more effectively and to produce concise and clear minutes, as this part of the role of assistant is as active as ever.

Please note that the book is written in British English, not American English.

Throughout this book the term 'assistant' is used to encompass various roles and titles for which this book is relevant, such as personal assistant, executive assistant, secretary, management assistant and office manager.

This book is written on the understanding that you are already proficient in all technical areas and in computer programs such as Word, Excel, Outlook/diary, contact databases and PowerPoint, and are aware of all new technology. This book is about life skills that will enrich your working life, enabling you to build excellent working relationships and exceed expectations of peers, superiors and yourself!

The *Definitive Personal Assistant & Secretarial Handbook*, second edition, will be your most knowledgeable friend; it will act as a reference book full of insights, tips, tools and earned wisdom for you to dip in and out of when looking for inspiration, support and answers. You will learn insights and top tips learnt from years of experience. It is written for those who want to make their unique boss–assistant relationship a resounding success built on mutual trust, which means that work output will excel, careers will flourish, relationships will succeed and communication skills will be exceptional, not to mention the bottom line of the company increasing. With successful working habits and therefore successful relationships, readers will look forward to going to work in the knowledge that they will enjoy the interaction, output and outcome of every day's endeavours. They will feel enormous satisfaction from the job they do, and will most likely have fun too!

In Appendix 1 you will find the 'Personal strengths assessment form' where you can learn about yourself and understand what your strengths are. It will also give you the opportunity to work on any weaknesses. After reading the appropriate chapters in the book to help with any areas you want to improve on, you will find help with goal setting in Chapter 3 and a structure to complete your goals.

This book will help you learn how to create a mutually effective working relationship that is productive and successful. It will provide an insight into your bosses' minds so that you can empathize and become the best assistant you can be.

There is a chapter for bosses and assistants to share so that bosses will understand better what is expected of them, how to treat and interact with assistants in order to help both parties create the most effective and efficient working relationship.

You will learn about the importance of attitudes, empowerment and mutually working together for the benefit of each other and the company you work for. This reference book will give you top tips on making the boss–assistant relationship work, telling you everything you need to know to be able to influence and communicate to the best of your ability and to develop successful, productive, effective and professional working relationships.

Throughout the book you will find many quotes, tips and advice from assistants, taken from a questionnaire that has been distributed to thousands of assistants throughout the world. Keep this book handy and accessible so that you can dip in and out of it when you feel the need for a helping hand or a coach to help you in your daily tasks and work relationships.

The book can be used as part of a training programme or during an induction process for an assistant or when growing into a new role. It can also be used to open up communications; to help the flow of communication and building of relationships so as to create effective and productive working partnerships.

All the forms used in this book can be downloaded, saved and printed as tools to use to help you be an exceptionally efficient and effective personal/executive assistant secretary. Please go to:

www.suefrance.com using the password GH49kv4 or
http://www.koganpage.com/editions/definitive-personal-assistant-secretarial-handbook/9780749465766

Relationship management

Understand yourself before you try to understand others

In order to build excellent, effective relationships and understand others, it is important that you understand yourself first.

To find out your strengths and weaknesses, complete the 'Personal strengths assessment' form in Appendix 1. Once you have completed it and transferred your scores, you will have an overall picture of how you perceive yourself. You can pat yourself on the back for the areas where you are confident and competent, and you should plan to concentrate on any weaknesses by reading this book and setting goals. In Chapter 3 you can learn how to set 'SMARTER' goals and objectives (see Appendix 4 for an explanation of SMARTER goals and a pro forma for goal setting).

When you realize what your strengths are, the next step is to learn how to articulate them to other people so that they know what you are capable of. However, be careful not to boast; simply articulate. For example, you may be good at languages and available for translation or you could be good at taking minutes, so offer your services, or you may be good at shorthand and could run workshops for your colleagues.

Find out what your boss's weaknesses are and make them your strengths so that you can complement them.

Something you need to be aware of: it is possible that a strength that is on the high end of the scale can sometimes be perceived as a weakness; for example, someone who appears to have lots of confidence may be perceived as being unapproachable or even arrogant. Someone who likes to have fun and may laugh a lot at work may be perceived as being flippant and not taken seriously. Therefore, when you are realizing what your strengths are, make sure you are aware that the strength could be perceived as a weakness in certain circumstances.

Appendix 2 features a 'Personal development plan' pro forma. It should be used to help you to understand yourself better, and to help you focus on your personal development/learning and training requirements. It will help you identify gaps in your skills and experience, and find ways to fill them. You will be able to reflect on past experiences and focus on learning outcomes; the end product will be that you will be motivated, your self-confidence will be boosted and your self-esteem will be much higher. This should lead to a satisfying and successful career as well as excellent working relationships. You can use this personal development plan in your appraisal meetings and to help you in career management.

What the boss–assistant relationship means to your health and well-being

It is important to get the boss–assistant relationship right because, emotionally, we are most affected by intimate relationships and power relationships. The power relationship in your life is with your boss; assistants probably spend more time with their bosses than the bosses do with their spouses. A bad relationship with a boss could cause anxiety, unhappiness, stress-related problems and even a risk of depression/illness. It is one of the top reasons why people leave their jobs. It can also cause physical symptoms such as high blood pressure.

Relationship building is a two-way process – you should take control of the situation and influence your boss(es) to agree to make the relationship work; Chapter 10 can be shared with your boss and used to build an effective working relationship. Whether you work for one or more bosses, you need to communicate constantly with each of them individually.

Image, perception and first impressions

Relationship management starts as soon as you meet someone. People make up their minds about each other in the first few seconds of meeting, so it is extremely important to make the right impression. Those first impressions last and can decide whether you get what you want from your meeting and perhaps even make the difference between getting a job or not!

The impact you make will be judged (consciously and subconsciously) on the basis of both verbal and non-verbal communication. It is important to note that 93 per cent of the way you come across to other people is determined by your tone of voice, attitude and body language, which includes how confident you appear to be, your behaviour and your appearance.

> Bill Docherty MBE (trainer, coach and my ex-boss) says: 'We have an internal physical filter and when we see people react in a certain way we will mentally note how they hold their heads, where they look, how they hold their shoulders, shake hands and how they make use of space. Our subconscious mind sifts through all the memories and experiences of different people we have encountered in our lives. As we do this we will pick out people who are similar and remember how they acted and what they were like and how we felt about them. We will then take this combined knowledge and feelings, bring it forward and attach it to the people we are meeting.'

Tone of voice

It is really important to speak with the right tone of voice and show the right attitude so that people want to be around you and enjoy your company. If your tone suggests a condescending attitude, boredom or anger, you will lose respect and people will no longer want to spend time speaking with you or listening to what you have to say.

Attitude

When you wake up in the morning you can choose to have a 'can do'/'can be'/'will do' happy attitude to work, to motivate yourself and say 'I'm really looking forward to work today and am eager to get started.' If you think you cannot do something then you probably won't be able to do it. You have to tell your subconscious mind that you can do whatever you put your mind to and you will be able to do it.

An assistant can succeed at almost anything for which they have unlimited enthusiasm and tenacity!

The alternative is to choose an attitude of 'I really don't want to go to work today, I just can't be bothered!' Which attitude do you think will help you enjoy work more? Remember – you have a choice of how you are going to respond to any situation.

Attitude also includes aiming for a healthy work–life balance and you should beware of spending too much time at work and not enough time with your family and friends. Always have time for yourself too – this is important because you won't be saying on your deathbed 'I wish I'd gone into work more.'

Positive beliefs and intentions followed by positive actions create positive results.

Here are four things you can do to make sure that you have the most positive attitude possible under any circumstance. They will also help to reduce stress and to build effective relationships:

- Focus on the future (rather than on the past), whatever challenge you face, including conflict. Instead of worrying about who did what and who is to blame, focus on where you want to be and what you want to do.

- Focus on the solution whenever you're faced with a difficulty. Do not waste your time and energy reflecting on the problem, whose fault it is or why it happened. Solutions are positive and problems are negative. As soon as you think in terms of solutions, you become a positive, proactive assistant.

- Look for the good in things and the positive side of any situation.

- Look for the valuable lesson in things; if something goes wrong or you make a mistake – what can you learn from it?

Managing your state of mind

You can manage your state of mind before you enter a room to make a great first impression, thereby creating self-confidence and being prepared for any meeting where you feel you need to influence and persuade.

If you are feeling nervous before you enter the room, take several deep breaths to get the oxygen circulating around your body and you will instantly feel calmer. You can manage your state of mind by thinking of a time when you have been particularly successful and full of confidence in either a business or personal situation. You should think back to that time and recreate the feeling you had then. Think about how you were standing and where your breathing was coming from (probably the abdomen). What were you thinking? What did you see and hear? How did you feel? You should fully experience how you felt in the past experience and keep those feelings of success and confidence when you enter the room and during your meeting.

Before you enter the room, relax your facial muscles as it is impossible to feel anxious when your muscles are relaxed, and when you enter the room your smile will appear genuine. Your eyes should be smiling as well as your mouth – if it is not a genuine smile then you will not be trusted. It is impossible to feel sad when you smile, and smiling is contagious as people will always smile back. Smiling shows a pleasant personality and people like to be around people who are happy. Smiling will help you to appear warm, open, friendly, confident and approachable – even when feeling nervous.

As you confidently knock on the door and walk in, you should hold your head up, put your shoulders back and smile as you look into the eyes of the people in the room. If there is only one person then focus on that person. If, however, you enter a room with your head down, avoiding eye contact, you may be considered as lacking in self-confidence. Remember to breathe deeply, making sure it is not shallow breathing in the upper chest, which is where you breathe when feeling anxious and stressed.

Visualization techniques are used by top athletes to help get them in the right frame of mind for any situation where they want to succeed. You should visualize yourself entering confidently into the room, having a successful meeting, getting on well with the boss and building instant rapport with ease and confidence. Finish by visualizing the feeling that you have got what you wanted out of the meeting. The feeling that you get from that is amazing, and when you believe in yourself you can make it happen.

The handshake

When you first meet your boss, clients or colleagues, you should shake hands in the most effective way as this makes a deep impression on people. You should confidently offer your hand to shake while still maintaining eye contact. Good eye contact is paramount (taking culture into consideration) – you cannot engage with someone properly if you are looking above their heads, down at the floor or over their shoulder. When shaking hands, make sure that you make contact at the crux between your thumb and forefinger (and not the ends of fingers) and that the handshake is strong and confident, with a gentle pumping up and down of the arms once or twice at most. Be sure not to squeeze the other person's hand too tightly or hurt them by digging rings into fingers. Do not have your hand too limp or it will give the impression that you have no confidence. (However, if the other person has a limp handshake, do take into consideration that there may be reasons other than lack of confidence, for example arthritis.)

Also remember to acknowledge the etiquette of handshaking of different cultures, where it may not be appropriate at all.

Professional image

To help build effective relationships, gain respect and encourage people to listen to you, it is important to act professionally and look professional. The image you portray influences the way you are perceived by other people (which may not always be the way you perceive yourself to be!). You need to manage the way you are perceived by managing your image, as the way you look and act is an extension of who you are and how you feel.

Good manners as well as polite, attentive and courteous behaviour will help build effective and satisfying relationships.

 Remember: the expression you wear is just as important as the clothes you wear.

Appearance

Appearance can speak volumes about your attitude and is a form of non-verbal communication that others will use to make up their minds about you. Even if your company has a casual dress policy, you are often the face of the organization, especially if you have to meet and greet clients, and you should always think about how you will be perceived and therefore how the company is being perceived. Any sign of dirty or scuffed shoes, untidy, greasy or dishevelled hair, creased clothes, stains, dirty nails or mismatched clothes could make a long-lasting negative impression. Even bitten nails may give the perception of your being a nervous type of person. Choice of clothes, hairstyles, jewellery (including body piercings) or anything to do with appearance can be considered a means of non-verbal communication.

Dressing well can affect your attitude, make you feel good and increase your self-esteem, and when your self-esteem is high your energy levels are increased and you become more productive. You may have to chair meetings and give presentations at work, and being smartly dressed gives you more confidence in those tasks – some people call it power dressing. Choice of colours is also important – choose the ones that suit you, as certain colours can make you look insignificant and even ill, whereas others can bring out the best in you and make you look attractive, dynamic and powerful.

Appropriate dress also varies between countries and cultures, so you should pay particular attention when in an unfamiliar setting or country. Make sure you know the traditions and norms.

Sue Robson, who is English but works in Saudi Arabia, says: 'In the Middle East, it is important that local culture is respected, especially with regard to dress code. For example, wearing a sleeveless top in a UK office is fine, especially in hot weather, whereas in the Middle East this would be totally unacceptable. During the month of Ramadan, it is particularly important to dress conservatively.'

Flirting

Being professional at all times includes not flirting in the office. It's okay to banter and have a laugh now and again but you must understand how far you can take this and know where to draw the line. One way to deal with 'serious' approaches is just to laugh them off. That helps to keep good professional working relationships and everyone saves face and keeps their jobs! At office parties don't drink too much, as it lowers your inhibitions and common sense has been known to fly out of the window! Almost all bosses (92 per cent) will remember such indiscretions, and although 74 per cent of them take it in the spirit of things, it could still ruin your reputation and possible chances of promotion.

The beginning of a business relationship

Your organization should offer you an induction where you can begin to learn about the business. If they don't have such a procedure and you are just thrown in at the deep end, make it your business to get your own induction, and later to take on a project for putting an induction procedure and binder together (as a new joiner you will know exactly what is needed). This will exceed expectations and help others – you will also quickly become an 'expert' on the company and you will be respected for your endeavours by your boss and peers.

In order to do your job effectively and to understand your boss's needs, study the culture of your new organization, talk to many different people and find out all you can about the business and the industry you work in. Study the technological words and abbreviations, policies and practices of your company. You will need to learn all about the protocol, processes and systems in place and obtain any relevant training to help you fulfil your role.

> *"One of the most important things you can do is to keep well informed and up to date about the business sector you work in, trends in your company and changes in technology."*
> (Gillian Richmond, past European chairman for EUMA)

Identify people who can help you in your role, and start building your network of relationships at work. Find opportunities to interact and get to know people. You should spend time with them either by organizing a meeting or by spending a lunch or coffee break with them. When you interact with your new colleagues, be friendly and approachable, showing a genuine interest in their work, and think about the impression you are making.

You can bring in your own experiences and expertise in areas that you could possibly improve on. You may look at things differently from the ways they have always been done. However, you should be flexible; adapt some of your ways and compromise on some areas if your boss/organization stipulates the way certain things have to be done.

> *"I believe our role is to assist the boss in whatever ways we can, in order to free them for more billable work. I think we need to drop our attitude of not wanting to do menial tasks, such as answering the phones, opening and date-stamping mail, even getting water or coffee for the boss, and so on. Screening calls can greatly help a boss's concentration."*
> (Janita C Sullivan, president, Legal Secretaries International Inc)

What is expected of each other: setting down the parameters

When you start working with a new boss you need to make a conscious decision to plan a successful working relationship by sitting down with him or her, deciding on how you want to work together and starting the process of really getting to know one another. Each relationship will differ and you need to agree the parameters and boundaries of acceptable behaviour and what you expect of each other. It is of paramount importance that you continually communicate with your boss(es) and with colleagues. The only way to succeed in an effective working relationship is to know and understand the rules and barriers that you have for each other; these may change in different situations and therefore constant communication is the key!

Respectfully tell your bosses what you expect of them, discuss what they expect of you, and endeavour to exceed their expectations!

Be clear about your boss's expectations and write down everything that is expected of you, by when and how. This is important so that you don't forget, but also so that if you are off work for any reason someone can pick up your work sheet and immediately see and understand what is expected of them.

Discuss how information will be shared and decisions made. How does your boss want you to deal with e-mails, post, telephone calls, the diary and clients? Can you set meetings in the diary without checking with the boss first? Do they use reminder systems and in and out trays? You may want to suggest ways of working that you have found particularly useful in your experience in other roles. Ask your boss which elements of your skills, knowledge and experience they felt would add value when they offered you the job so that you can fulfil their vision of you adding value.

Find out what motivates your boss, what their values are, what annoys them, what stresses them, what preferences they have, what can help with any moods they may get, whether they can be contacted when on holiday and what outside-work activities they do. Are there any days when you have to make sure the diary is clear for them to get away on time? Maybe they like to go to the gym at lunchtime on some days, so make sure this is put in the diary. Their work–life balance is just as important as yours.

When you are having a meeting with them and letting them know of your expectations, let them know of any days when you definitely cannot stay late – for instance if you are taking children to activities or attending evening class – so that they know in advance and can organize themselves around it. Remember also to remind them on the day you have to leave on time. Also remind them first thing in the morning and then an hour or so before you have to leave and make sure you do leave so that they know you mean it. Then the next time they will make sure they get the information to you on a timely basis! 'Mean what you say and say what you mean!'

You should also discuss any training requirements that you have and try to gain agreement for you to attend secretarial workshops, webinars, conferences and exhibitions so that you can continually learn and develop yourself.

Ask about joining secretarial networks such as EUMA, and try to get an agreement for your company to pay your subscription as well as your monthly fee for the meetings. They should realize the benefit you will gain from belonging to such a group in terms of self-development and networking. You would be the face of your company when attending meetings, and business opportunities may arise.

You should also find out about your new boss's family; it's helpful to have a list of emergency numbers, such as spouse's work/mobile number, doctors, dentists, schools and nanny if appropriate.

Discuss how you might lighten the boss's workload and be empowered to do some project work. See more on empowerment in Chapter 10, 'A chapter to share with your boss'.

> *"Our relationship works because we invest time and energy to make it work. We share the same core values – trust, openness, honesty, fairness; strive to balance family life and work life; know our boundaries. It's about flexibility, tolerance and partnership."*
> (Jan Foxcroft (assistant) and Peter Lawrence (manager))

Key attributes, skills and knowledge that bosses look for in an assistant

> *"A good assistant is your public face and your representative, so their style and the way they project their image needs to mirror yours in terms of customer service, values, work ethic."*
> (Carol Ritchie, finance director)

- To display excellent interpersonal and communication skills with the boss, with clients, all levels of staff and fellow assistants, whether face to face, on the phone or by e-mail.
- To be trustworthy, confidential and loyal.
- To be a confidant.
- To be wholly committed to doing the job right and to the best of your ability.
- To have the ability to understand the boss's thinking and management style, so that you can make decisions without needing to check with him or her.
- To use active listening skills (the assistant is often the only person the boss trusts!).
- To take ownership: be proactive and anticipate problems and try to solve them.
- To be able to sort out difficult situations and problems without asking your boss to sort them for you.
- To keep cool, calm and effective during very busy and deadline-driven times – be like a swan! Even if you are paddling like mad under the water (to get everything done in the right way in the right time), be calm and serene above the water so everyone around you perceives that you are in control.
- To be full of energy and enthusiasm.
- To be organized, with a flexible attitude.
- To be persuasive and assertive.
- To take on more responsibility wherever the opportunity arises.
- To provide empathy and support.
- To be a team worker – helping others and delegating effectively.
- To forgive your boss for being less than perfect, and not to dwell on the negatives.
- To motivate each other and bounce ideas off each other.
- To have a sense of humour.

> *"To succeed as an assistant, the most important thing is loyalty!!! Both to your boss and of course to the company. You also need to be social and develop your own network within your company and outside. Look after your health, work at a high speed, be creative and always be in a good mood and ready to challenge yourself!"*
>
> (Marie Voss, Winner of the 'The Golden Paper Clip' award at the annual Office Professionals Day 2011, Sweden)

Working styles

It is important from the outset to find out your boss's preferred ways of working and also to explain your own working styles so that you understand each other clearly. For example, you may like to use your own initiative and creative ideas or you may require clear guidelines and frameworks to function effectively. You may need to learn to adapt quickly to the style of your boss but eventually, with communication, empathy and understanding, you will know each other so well that you will each know how the other thinks and what either of you would do in any given situation.

Sometimes bosses and assistants work best when they complement each other's working styles; for instance, an extrovert, flamboyant and loud boss might be better suited to an assistant who is quieter, task focused and a calming influence. Sometimes relationships work best when people are similar; if a boss is a 'messy desk' person and so is the assistant, but they both know it works for them, then they understand it and will not get irritated by it. However, a 'messy desk' assistant should still keep their desk tidy and as clear as possible as then they will be perceived by everyone as being in control. If you work for more than one boss then you have to adapt to each one's management style. Some bosses think about the big picture and not the detail; when giving instructions they may not tell you all you need to know. Get clarification and ask questions, whether by talking to each other or texting or by e-mail.

Ultimately, it is your responsibility to fit in with your boss's preferred management style. You will not always agree with him or her and you can try to find better ways of working or compromise on certain things, but it may be a case of your learning how to adapt to their management style.

Constant communication

Train your boss to communicate with you regularly – this is crucial to the success of your relationship. You should know where your boss is at all times even though you may not reveal this to others.

Throughout your relationship it is imperative to have regular meetings and continuous communication – possibly every day, or whatever works for you both and complements your schedules.

The length and formality of the meetings are up to you and your boss. If you use an agenda, make sure that your boss has the opportunity to add anything they wish to discuss. Whatever the case, treat them like an important client meeting: have them in your boss's diary as often as you need in order to do your job properly. When you are in the meeting, shut the door and put the boss's phone through to someone to take messages so that you are not disturbed. Bosses who do not like doing administration will usher you out as soon as they can, but stick at it until you have all the answers you need that day. A good tip from Susie Baron-Stubley, (trainer) is to say at the end of the meeting to your boss: 'And what else is there you want to tell me?' Using the words 'what else' prompts them into thinking that there is indeed something else and they rack their brains until you do have everything they need to tell you.

"Never be frightened to ask your boss to explain again, if you don't understand. People would rather you do it right, than either totally wrong or not at all."

(Carole Rigney)

If you have a boss who spends a lot of time away from the office then suggest that they phone you after each meeting and update you on what has happened. You can make notes and take any follow-up action that is required. If all that is needed is a new date in the diary for a meeting with the client or an e-mail that needs sending with information, you can do it before your boss has even left the client's car park! Imagine how the client feels when your boss has promised something and, as soon as they have left the client's office, whatever has been promised is sitting in the client's inbox! You will have exceeded the expectations of your boss and the client.

Update meetings and telephone calls can be pivotal to an excellent working relationship. Assistants will feel more involved and have more understanding of their boss's world. Good news can also be shared, creating excitement and celebration that is always good for building relationships.

It is also important to take just a few minutes to catch up on things outside the office – such as your boss's home life and hobbies. When you understand the whole person, this helps to build relationships.

We all interpret things differently. If you are having a meeting with your boss and you want to ask for something, change something or have a suggestion to make – or even want to take on more of the boss's work – then state what you want clearly and get to the point, backing it up with data, reasons and proof if appropriate. Choose your time to approach the boss in a suitable location such as their office; don't do it whilst they are passing your desk or as you pass in the corridor. If necessary, book yourself a time in the diary and go into the boss's room.

Bosses may have opinions about your performance but fail to share those thoughts. Initiating occasional feedback discussions and making sure your appraisals happen will give them an opportunity to let you know what they are thinking – see more information on appraisals in the section on 'Continual learning' in Chapter 3.

You may encounter 'difficult people' or characteristics that you do not like; however, you should be consistently professional, pleasant and cooperative regardless of how difficult or unpleasant they may be. You should always show respect for other people even if you don't like them. Be patient and get to know people and 'their ways' and take a look at Chapter 4 on 'Dealing with difficult people and managing conflict'.

Assumptions

People make assumptions, rightly or wrongly. You should ask questions to ensure clarity. You may assume people want you to do something in a certain way; you may assume they don't mind you coming in five or 10 minutes late every so often; you may assume that you know what they are thinking and what they want. Once you have been working for someone for a long time you can often be correct in assumptions, but sometimes you can be wrong!

Make sure your actions and decisions are founded on facts and reality as much as humanly possible, especially when under pressure. Always establish the facts, check the validation of your assumptions and take time to reason things through so that you don't make mistakes.

Be proactive, anticipate needs, be prepared and exceed expectations

To be a successful assistant you have to be willing, able, flexible and proactive. Think ahead and plan, carry out tasks before they are required, anticipate problems and try to solve them. Use quieter periods to pre-empt requests. Be organized and prepared in advance (including updating and organizing paperwork and files). A successful assistant deals with as much as possible to prevent it landing on the boss's desk, and endeavours to always exceed expectations.

"Whenever a VIP programme was under way, it was almost a rule that you expected something unexpected. To avoid problems I would organize as much as possible in advance and provide for every possible contingency, by having IT staff on standby and so on. Then when something unexpected cropped up I could deal with it calmly and effectively."
(Liz O'Farrell)

"Eighty per cent of your boss's headaches come from 20 per cent of activities and everything else runs along smoothly, so get rid of that bottom 20 per cent and you will be perceived as a super assistant and your boss will be a lot happier. Give solutions not problems – answers not questions."
(Bill Docherty MBE)

To generalize somewhat, male bosses often prefer to focus on one solution at a time rather than having to choose between a range of options. Female bosses, on the other hand, may prefer to be given several options to choose from.

Know your capabilities and don't promise anything you cannot deliver. It is especially important to be proactive when you are working for more than one boss and if you are working to a deadline. You should inform your boss(es), without having to be chased for information, and report back if you think you are not going to make deadlines they give you (but try to get help from colleagues first). Let your bosses know in good time as they may be able to extend the deadline, and being forewarned enables them to do something about a problem.

Try to make your boss look good and never show disrespect for him or her in front of anyone. Produce high-quality documents and presentations, and meet deadlines. Make sure you return calls as promised, and remind your boss of what they have to do on a timely basis. If you have any problems that need solving, address them. Contribute new ideas and suggestions.

To help you to be prepared you should check the diary for the coming week and month, making sure that you have prepared all the necessary papers for each meeting. You should also prepare maps if required and diarize time for any preparation work, as well as organizing any travel that is required (arranging hotel bookings, visas and foreign currency, making sure passports are up to date and so on). When booking travel, make sure you know any preferences your boss has (eg aisle or window seat preference). You should also note any allergies that your boss may have when booking restaurants and meals in hotels, and know what type of accommodation is preferred.

Being proactive is also about grasping opportunities when they arise, such as volunteering to take responsibility for projects that you realize can save your boss some time as well as giving yourself a challenge and a chance to increase your skill set. You should take ownership of your work and projects and add value to your boss and your company. By assuming more responsibility for tasks, projects and processes, you will become an increasingly valuable asset in the relationship between you and your boss.

> *"Read everything that comes across your desk, ask questions, and keep on learning. Become involved, and be pushy about getting answers if necessary. Bosses love to tell you about their work – they are just often too busy or don't realize the secretary cares to learn about it."*
>
> (Janita C Sullivan)

Be accountable: take pride in a high standard of work

You should maintain a high-level professional service to all people with whom you interact outside and inside the company. It is important that your grammar and spelling are correct as the standard of the documentation, whether it is hard copy or e-mail, is important (it is evidence of the company's professionalism and high standards). Using the spell checker on the computer is not sufficient as it does not pick up homophones (words that sound the same yet are spelt differently and mean different things, eg their and there). It is important to read your work for sense and grammar, whether it will be sent out internally or externally. Be very careful when you are proof reading as it is easy to miss spelling mistakes and transposed letters.

> If you read your documents from bottom up and backwards you are likely to pick up any spelling mistakes. Read it forwards to make sure that the grammar makes sense and the words flow correctly.

Try to get a fresh pair of eyes to look over your work and you do the same for them.

A poem to remember grammar rules is supplied by Jade Hall, who smartly suggests having it on your desktop as a reminder:

The 9 Parts of Speech

ARTICLES are 3 little words that work with a noun
They are *a* word, *an* elephant and *the* town

A noun's the name of anything
As *field* or *fountain*, *school* or *swing*

Instead of nouns, the PRONOUNS stand –
Her head, *his* face, *your* arm, *my* hand

ADJECTIVES describe the 'kind of noun'
As *great*, *small*, *pretty*, *white* or *brown*

The VERB means action, something done –
To *read*, to *write*, to *jump*, to *run*

How things are done, the ADVERBS tell
As *quickly*, *slowly*, *badly*, *well*

The PREPOSITION shows relation
As *in* the street, or *at* the station

CONJUNCTIONS join, in many ways
Sentences, words, *or* phrase *and* phrase

The INTERJECTION creates the spark!
For the exclamation mark!'

Through poetry we learn the 9 parts of speech
Which reading, writing and speaking teach

Make sure that your business writing is up to date, for example:

- Use active not passive voice (ie the subject of the sentence does the action of the sentence, eg 'The finance director signed off the accounts' as opposed to 'The accounts were signed off by the finance director' which is passive – where the subject of the sentence receives the action).

- Use bold and no underlines (unless it is in track changes).

- Keep it short and simple (KISS) because shorter sentences are easier to understand. Avoid redundant phrases, for example 'I am writing to...' (they know you are writing!).

- Choose simple and short words instead of long old-fashioned words. This is most useful in our multicultural society where English may not be the reader's first language, for example instead of 'terminates' write 'ends', instead of 'commence' write 'start' etc...

- Replace old-fashioned phrases with one word, for example 'I should be obliged if you would...' with 'Please...' or 'In the event that...' with 'If...' etc...

- Use modern terminology; for example, instead of 'Please do not hesitate to contact me if you require any further information' use 'Please let me know if you have any questions' or instead of 'Attached please find...' use 'I attach ...'. Instead of 'Please respond...' it should be 'Please reply...' etc

- The modern text language should not be used in business documents; 'u r getting l8ter and l8ter LOL' is strictly a no-go area in business writing.

Empathy

Study bosses carefully to get to know their wants, needs and goals, to put yourself in their shoes. Seek to understand the pressures they are under and empathize with them, then see what you can do to alleviate pressures and solve problems. Bosses have clients, peers, subordinates and possibly their own bosses to answer to, and they may well have more than one crisis going on at any one time. Be prepared to work overtime if necessary and volunteer to do this on occasions when you know it would be appreciated. This will work in your favour, as when you need time off work it is more likely that your boss will agree to it (the law of reciprocation is quite powerful).

If there is any part of their job that you can do, you should volunteer to take on the project – take on more responsibility to ease the pressures on the boss. If they can delegate, take the work on – it makes your job more interesting and more rewarding and adds to your curriculum vitae.

From Sue Robson: 'When bosses arrive at the office, either first thing in the morning or when returning from meetings, don't stop them as they pass your desk to give them their messages and so on. Give them a few minutes to settle in instead of demanding immediate attention and they will be far more receptive towards you.'

Always treat others as you wish to be treated – it's common good manners. Treat people with respect and courtesy that they deserve and you will be treated with respect too.

Honesty and integrity

When mistakes are made many people are reluctant to apologize, fearing that admitting fault will harm their reputation, result in punishment or simply make them look foolish.

'Honesty is the best policy' to repair a situation, so if you make a mistake – own up (it is better than being found out) but first try to solve any problems that may arise. Then let people know what you have done, that you are sorry about it, and how you have tried to solve it. Owning up also prevents you from becoming stressed and worried about the problem. We all have bad days and we all make mistakes, and if some blame lies with you – accept it. A properly phrased and well-timed apology makes you look stronger, not weaker, by showing that you have the courage to admit your mistakes. It will help towards repairing any damage to relationships.

Integrity encompasses honesty, trustworthiness and high moral values. It is vital that top assistants are seen to have integrity as they deal with highly confidential material and are trusted with information that perhaps only the chief executive officer and possibly the board have sight of. They are often the only people their bosses can confide in and can be used as a sounding board. Assistants should have a strong belief in their high moral values and the boss should be able to trust them.

Trust

"Knowing and mastering everything that is important to my boss, always staying on top of everything. Knowing his next move before he has even contemplated making it himself. I keep my boss's whole existence in my hands and the only person who knows the full extent of it is my boss. Not only does he discuss extremely sensitive and confidential business matters with me but we also talk about more private matters. He knows that I am to be trusted 100 per cent."

(Eila Sandberg)

Trust, respect and discretion are really important in any relationship. You both have to be able to trust each other and this has to be earned over time by doing what you promise, by being honest and open in your relationship, by communicating effectively and by owning up to mistakes.

Bosses should be able to trust you to get on with your work even though they are not there, and be confident that you will follow all the correct procedures and policies and be as productive as you can. Quite often they don't know the policies themselves and if they can trust that you are well informed and know what you are doing, then it's something less for them to think about.

Trust means:

- not laying any blame;
- producing the results expected;
- providing honest feedback;
- discussing problems directly;
- not talking behind people's backs;
- doing a fair share of the work;
- meeting agreed deadlines;
- sharing information and knowledge that you need;
- giving credit where it is due.

If someone 'betrays' your trust – check your assumptions. 'Betrayal' implies that someone either intentionally did something that you did not expect or failed to do something that you did expect. If you believe a colleague has disclosed confidential information, for example, you should check your assumptions: did you clearly state that it was not to be discussed?

Keeping promises helps gain trust and respect. If you promise to call someone back by a certain time, then do so. They will remember you because few people actually do that.

Office politics

Typically, we use the term 'office politics' to describe our colleagues' behaviour (never our own) as scheming and manipulating, whereas when we do it we are building relationships, developing strategies, and communicating!

Many people feel that office politics involves devious plotting or blatant self-promotion and even 'back stabbing'. However, in reality, politics is what naturally happens whenever people with different goals, interests and personalities try to work together. The process itself is simply a fact of office life.

To succeed, we not only have to do outstanding work, but also to deal with quirky bosses and colleagues with difficult and annoying characteristics. Colleagues get defensive when we point out their mistakes, unscrupulous rivals try to stab us in the back, and managers make decisions that seem totally unfair. Managing the political environment is just as important as managing tasks and responsibilities. Politics is about getting what you want by influencing others (some may call it manipulating).

Good office politics includes raising your profile in the office and the industry you work in. Success at work depends on both results and 'strategic' relationships with, for example, your boss, your boss's boss, the assistant of your boss's boss, the human resource manager, IT department and of course the assistants of your clients and clients themselves. Be your boss's eyes and ears. When you hear of something they may need to act upon, then it is your duty to let them know.

How to manage your boss

> Successful assistants have patience, empathy and understanding, and are able to manage upwards. Sometimes it is useful to be thick skinned; remember never to take it personally when bosses are venting off!

We cannot always choose the bosses we work with. Sometimes we 'inherit' them, sometimes they are 'given' to us, perhaps through a change in management; sometimes we may even have chosen them, but it's not until we work with them that we find out what they are really like.

The frustrations that assistants can experience when dealing with untrained, inexperienced bosses with inappropriate management styles can cause stress, sleepless nights, headaches and anxiety and may even cause staff to be off work ill and ultimately to leave.

We have to make the most of the bosses we have and some of us are luckier than others. So the more effectively you can manage your boss, the better your relationship will be and the more you are likely to enjoy work and your profession. The less skilful your boss is at managing down, then the more important it is for you to be able to manage up!

Tips on managing up:

- Assistants should take the responsibility for improving the relationship and getting the buy-in of their boss. They should also accept any shortcomings a boss may have – no one is perfect; we all have our off days and possibly annoying habits too. You can help bosses to realize what their shortcomings are and help them to improve. This may just mean sitting down and talking to them openly, but you must be tactful about the way you approach this. Sometimes it is prudent to recognize what annoys and upsets your boss and avoid whatever it is! If your boss is having an off day, then keep out of the way and try not to antagonize them.

- You should manage the expectations of bosses. If they are expecting too much of you – for example if you are continually having to come in early, work through lunch and stay late – then you have to ask for a meeting and let them know the situation. Don't forget to offer a solution to the problem. You need to be assertive but never aggressive. Know when to say no (calmly and courteously) and explain your thinking as to why you have said no. Be tactful and diplomatic.

- Most bosses like to hear new ideas and approaches. Share your thoughts about how to improve your relationship, your role, processes, customer service or the work environment.

- Give your boss a sincere compliment when appropriate and when you need to give constructive criticism then, at an appropriate time, sit down with him or her and say there is something you wish to discuss and do it calmly – adult to adult.

- In the case of new managers who have never experienced working with an assistant before, keep in mind that the transition to management is difficult. You need to help them work with an assistant and guide them – this might include simple things like how to dictate correctly into a dictaphone, for instance the correct order to dictate a table and the need to spell out unusual names. They may be nervous or they may come across as arrogant because they simply don't know how to be with an assistant, and you can help them and work it out together – again it cannot be stressed enough that constant communication is key.

- You may start working with a boss who has come from another organization and requires help in settling in. You will need to help them by sharing information on new procedures, process and culture, and guide them on protocol. However, you have to respect the fact that they are experienced in management roles and you may have to work at adapting your work style to theirs. In some cases they may in fact have been brought in to change things. Be flexible, adaptable and open to change.

- If your company already does 360° appraisals, then great; if they don't then suggest that you start. Giving constructive feedback on a six-monthly basis goes a long way to helping your working relationship succeed as long as you both agree on this type of appraisal and action is taken on any outcomes.

- Ask your boss out to lunch so that you get to know him or her outside work; you could conduct constructive feedback on such an occasion.

Successfully managing upward will help make your time at work more pleasant, and make it easier to accomplish your goals, enjoy work and manage your relationships.

Your success depends upon partnering with your boss and building an effective working relationship. This can be achieved through constant communication and understanding of each other's boundaries and expectations. You should learn to understand yourself as well as understand your boss and be able to adapt to different communication and work styles that they exhibit. You should aim to be so in tune with your boss that you are able to represent them in various situations.

Timing and empathy are also important skills and you should be sensitive to your boss's needs and be aware of how and when to approach them.

You need to establish trust, credibility and proactively manage tasks that impact on your boss's productivity and enable the goals of the organization to be reached. Your professional image and the perception that others have of you depend on the high standards of work that you set for yourself and the skills and abilities that you exhibit in managing yourself and your boss. You should be accountable for the work you produce and recognize the value you bring to your role and be proud of what you do.

02 Communication skills

Conscious and subconscious communication skills are paramount to helping you build powerful, trusting and mutually successful relationships. Communication is important in all situations and in particular the situations where you can build first impressions:

- meetings;
- on the phone;
- networking;
- giving presentations;
- business conferences;
- e-mails;
- social occasions.

Body language

We all interpret body language subconsciously most of the time. Whenever you notice body language you must take everything into consideration and nothing in isolation – attitude, tone of voice, what is said, how people look when they say it, what they are trying to achieve when they are saying it and what their positive intention is. The better we know people, the better we can read their body language. Understanding non-verbal communication improves with practice.

Be aware that there are cultural differences in body language and gestures (such as waving and pointing), which could be open to misinterpretation. However, facial expressions for anger, fear, sadness and happiness are similar throughout the world.

Congruence

Your posture, facial expression, eye contact and non-verbal language speak louder than words. People 'listen' to body language more than the spoken words. Up to 93 per cent of communication effectiveness is determined by non-verbal behaviour. If you want to mask your true feelings or your immediate reaction to information, then you must be aware of your body language. You may have your voice and words under control but your body language, including micro facial expressions and movement, can give your true thoughts and feelings away. Therefore make sure that when you want to convey a message your body language is congruent with your words in order to give a clear impression and message.

If you are unsure what your boss is conveying to you owing to incongruence of body language and words, then ask questions or repeat back what you believe he or she actually means so as to clarify the situation.

Visual, auditory and kinaesthetic

According to theories of neuro-linguistic programming (NLP), there are three main ways that individuals process their thoughts and communication styles: visual, auditory and kinaesthetic. Once you understand these three characteristics you will be able to recognize each type and it will help you communicate more effectively, which in turn helps to build excellent rapport. By listening to others it is easy to detect which method they choose, and you should echo the other person (adopting their language patterns and styles and mirroring their body language). We all use all three communication styles but most of us have a preference for one or two of them.

You can tell whether people are visual, auditory or kinaesthetic by their body language and the language they use, as outlined below.

Visual

Visual people process their world by means of pictures and what they see, including the use of pictures in their decision making.

When visual people talk to you or when they are thinking, their eyes tend to look up (as they are looking at imaginary pictures in front of them in the air). They say things like: 'It looks good to me,' 'Show me what you mean,' 'I see what you mean,' 'Can you see what I mean?' 'I get the picture' and 'I can see it clearly now.'

Listen for words and expressions such as 'looks good', 'a bright idea', 'I'll paint a picture for you', 'bright', 'that's clear', 'vision' and 'colourful'.

Auditory

Auditory people process their world and arrive at their decisions by means of the words that are used and what they hear.

Their eyes often look to the side horizontally and they also put their head to one side while listening. They use language that has sound as the main component, like: 'Tell me more,' 'I hear what you say,' 'I'll talk to you later,' 'It was good to speak to you,' 'That sounds good,' 'Tell me again' and 'It rings a bell.' Auditory people will use expressions and words such as 'sounds good', 'clear as a bell', 'rings true' and 'loud'.

Kinaesthetic

Kinaesthetic people base their decisions on how they feel. They drop their eyes down towards the ground when you talk to them, and talk about how they feel: 'That feels right,' 'That makes me feel sad,' 'That makes me feel good,' 'I understand how you feel,' 'I feel you are worried about...' 'I feel as if you are uncomfortable...' 'I sense you're thinking about...' and so on.

Kinaesthetic people tend to hug themselves or touch their bodies in some way, like clasping hands or folding arms. In body language terms this can be seen as a barrier, but if you understand that these people may be kinaesthetic then you may change your perception of them.

As a word of warning: it is important to realize that if you see someone with their arms crossed, for example, it does not necessarily mean that they are defensive or angry or not interested – it may mean that they process their world kinaesthetically (feelings based) and like to hug themselves; it may even mean that they are feeling a bit cold. Remember to consider a number of signs/clues in order to come to a proper conclusion.

To find out how you prefer to process your world you can take a simple test that can be found in Appendix 3.

Matching and mirroring (reflecting)

'Matching and mirroring' is the term used for subtly adopting a pose and/or expression similar to the person you are talking to. As a result, the other person feels that you are 'on the same wavelength' and is likely to talk longer and share more information. When you do this you will find that you build rapport quickly and easily, as people like people whom they feel (subconsciously) are like them. You should match their energy, whether they cross or uncross their legs, how fast or slowly they speak, their tone of voice and even the way they are breathing (whether slow and deep or fast and shallow). It is good to leave a small gap before changing your posture to match theirs so as not to make it too obvious.

Matching and mirroring angry people

Some people shout when they get angry or are excited, or just as a habit. When matching and mirroring someone who is shouting and angry, you may match their tonality, speed, quality, loudness of voice (maybe a little lower) and body language, but do not copy their angry words or any threatening language they might use. Your gestures should be similar but not quite as flamboyant and not threatening. Once you begin to build rapport, start to bring down your own loudness, speed and so on, and they will follow.

Groups

Most groups have a leader. If you are conversing with a group of people, you should start by establishing rapport with the leader, using matching and mirroring, in order to build rapport with the whole group.

Tone of voice

Your tone of voice can let others know exactly how you are feeling as it shows your enthusiasm, attitude, lack of interest, or anger. Therefore if you wish to influence your boss you can show genuine enthusiasm and interest in something by using an animated tone of voice.

Once you have 'mirrored' for a while you will find that when you start changing your body posture the people you are talking to will follow your lead and this means that they feel comfortable with you; rapport develops and your relationship has begun. You may get a warm feeling in the pit of your stomach, and they may say things like 'I feel like I have known you for a long time' or 'I find it easy to talk to you,' and you will both feel easy with each other.

Make sure your mirroring is subtle, but also realize that this technique needs practising until you feel comfortable doing it.

Eye contact

Making very little eye contact can convey either shyness and submissiveness or that you have something to hide; it could also suggest that you feel superior or are not interested. You can use your eyes to express interest in other people or in your surroundings. Keeping eye contact makes you appear more confident in almost any situation. This is particularly true in job interviews where you want to appear interested, confident and calm.

On the other hand, if you stare and have too much eye contact it can seem confrontational or intimidating; in the natural process of talking to someone we do flick our eyes away when we are processing our thoughts.

When you are in a group of people, you should make sure you look at each person for a few seconds to make everyone feel included and imply respect for everybody in the group. If you are not comfortable with looking into people's eyes then you can look into the triangular area that ranges from the left eyebrow across to the right eyebrow and down to the nose and up to the left eyebrow again – when you look into this triangular area other people cannot tell if you are looking into their eyes or not, so it looks as if you are keeping eye contact.

If, when you walk into a room, you look around, you will give out the impression of somebody who cares about where they are – and people will be more likely to approach you. If you keep your eyes averted (as is common if you are nervous) then you will look as if you would rather be somewhere else and appear less approachable and not confident.

When you keep eye contact you will be able to 'read' other people's body language and facial expressions. You may realize that you need to change what you are saying if they look as if they do not agree, or that you need to explain more if they have a quizzical expression on their face. If you are not looking at them you will not pick up any signals.

Eye movement will tell you whether they are thinking about the future or the past. When people look to the right they are creating and thinking about the future and when they look to the left they are remembering and thinking about the past. The eye movement may not be exaggerated – it could be minute – but if you look carefully you will begin to recognize it. By looking at people's eyes you can see if they are telling lies or not, because if you ask them a factual question and they look to their right they are about to make something up or exaggerate. If they look to their left they are going to tell you the truth, as they are accessing their past. However, you should note that there is a small group of left-handed people where the eye movements are reversed.

Use of space

People have a 'personal space', which is also an important type of non-verbal communication and we should take notice of it. If you go up to someone who then takes a step back, respect that as indicating the personal space that the person needs. The amount of distance we need is different for each of us, depending on how comfortable we feel when someone is standing in front of us. It also depends on the situation we are in and the level of familiarity.

The 'influential' right side

Bill Docherty MBE, master practitioner in NLP and my ex-boss, has spent over 30 years teaching negotiation techniques and has found that the majority of people are more easily influenced when you stand or sit on their right-hand side.

Body language and non-verbal behaviour account for 93 per cent of the perceived impact that you have on people. When you go for an interview or when you want to influence people, try to make sure you sit slightly to their right even if it means moving your chair a little (and even if you are across the table from them), so that they have to move their eyes and/or head slightly to their right to look at you. Being on their right puts you in their perceived future (and not their past!). When you are trying to make an impression, move your chair away from the desk to create space around you.

Hands

Hands are also very expressive. Open gestures, such as moving your hands away from your body, resting them on your lap palm upwards or on the desk in front of you, including exposing wrists, make you appear open and honest. Making too many hand gestures can make you appear nervous and uncontrolled, which is especially worth remembering when attending interviews.

Avoid putting your hand over your mouth or wringing your hands together or touching your sleeves – these gestures can make you appear tense, nervous, and sometimes dishonest. However, when reading other people's body language, remember that you have to take account of a range of clues to come to a conclusion about someone. For example, some people may cover their mouths when speaking to you, but that could be because they don't like the way their teeth look, or it could just have become a habit.

Posture

You can use your posture to communicate that you are interested, open, honest and confident. By facing someone, you appear attentive and look as if you are listening to them – particularly when you lean forwards slightly. By facing away from the other person or leaning back, you show a lack of interest. However, you should be careful not to appear aggressive when facing someone and bear in mind the importance of personal space.

How to influence the 'chemistry' between you and your boss

One of the main strategies for gaining mutual respect is to have constant verbal (and non-verbal), open and honest communication between you and your boss. In that way you both know what is going on at all times, and understand each other and your respective needs. The boss will gain trust in you, your abilities and decision-making powers so that he or she can trust you to make decisions and handle matters in their absence if required.

E-mail communication

"If you have access to your boss's e-mail account I would suggest you regularly read the e-mails, even if the boss deals with them themselves. It is always useful to be well informed and to have a broad picture of what they are doing."

(Charlotte Beffert)

It is also a good idea to read your boss's sent e-mails so that you know what they have answered, enabling you to understand what is happening with your boss's work.

All e-mails should give a professional impression and be written with good business English and grammar. They should be logically laid out using paragraphs, headings and bullet points with concise, clear and accurate writing. E-mails should be kept short and simple, using everyday words.

Remember to put a heading in the subject in your e-mail. Everyone gets so much e-mail that they may scan their inbox for ones they feel they need to read urgently, so make the heading something that will entice them to open it and read it. They may use also the subject heading for filing their e-mails. It is important to remember that if you pick up an e-mail to reply to it, you need to change the subject heading if you are e-mailing about a different subject.

E-mails are easy to send but so difficult to retract (if at all), and when writing them you should carefully consider the tone and message conveyed. You must also make sure that they are sent to the correct recipients, with everyone copied in who should be. You may find it useful to use the option to allow you to delay sending an e-mail so that you have time to think about it before it actually goes.

The human eye finds it easier to read small letters rather than capitals, and capitals should be avoided as it is a form of 'SHOUTING'. Making words bold is useful to highlight headings and areas which you require to **stand out** from the rest.

Be careful when sending group e-mails that you do not give away people's e-mail addresses against their wishes. You should use blind copy (bcc) to keep the e-mail address of each recipient private.

Be careful how you word e-mails and how they read – think about how they will come across to the recipient. If you are angry about something, don't send off an e-mail in haste: think about it, draft it and go back to it later when you have calmed down; change it or delete it if necessary. Remember that it is sometimes better to pick up a phone or meet face to face, especially if the matter is a sensitive issue or a problem that can be resolved quickly and efficiently by speaking to each other. No one wants to get into an e-mail war which could end up as a disciplinary meeting or even a career move! At the least it could ruin a relationship.

E-mails that are quite curt, short and to the point are sometimes perceived as coming from someone who is abrupt or arrogant. They can irritate some people, even though you may be doing it this way because of lack of time. You should write an e-mail, then read it from the reader's point of view – imagine how the wording could be perceived and interpreted and what the consequences could be. Messages should always have a greeting at the beginning and be signed off at the end. It is a good idea to use 'signatures', which may include a farewell greeting such as 'kind regards or 'warm regards' and your full contact details to help the recipient should they want to call you.

Similarly, people do not want to receive long e-mails that ramble on but rather ones that are to the point. If it is necessary to give lots of information, this should be attached as a Word document rather than in the e-mail itself.

Be very careful with sending confidential information in e-mails as they can be forwarded on and can be read by the company if the authorities so wish. Consider whether it would be better to post or deliver highly confidential material by hand.

E-mail etiquette – five top tips by Dr Monica Seeley, international e-mail best practice expert.

Your goals should be: right message, right first time: this reduces the rounds of e-mail ping-pong as each party tries to work out what the other is saying. With this in mind, here are my five top tips for brilliant e-mail etiquette to save everyone time and embarrassment:

1 Always include a professional greeting and closing, eg Dear [name] and Kind regards, Best wishes.

2 Say what the main point of your e-mail is about in the first two lines. Add supporting information afterwards.

3 Write using clear, concise and grammatically correct language.

4 Think five. Keep your e-mail short: maximum, five questions and five sentences. Any longer and the recipient will lose interest.

5 Think ahead and include any information and questions which the recipient is likely to come back on.

For more tips like these see *Brilliant E-mail* by Monica Seeley.

Be aware of your company's e-mail etiquette. Use your personal e-mail address for personal e-mails rather than clogging up the company's inbox with your personal correspondence. Be careful not to use work time for your personal concerns.

Use the tools available to organize and manage your inbox effectively. Take time to find out what is available to help you be more efficient as you probably use only 20 per cent of them. For example, you can use the 'out of office' or auto responder not just when you are on holiday but also if you want to spend quality time on a project without interruption. You can let senders know that you will not be looking at your e-mails until, for example, 4.00 pm and give an alternative action for them to take in an emergency and perhaps redirect them to another person. That way you can get on with your other business without worrying that something urgent may be sitting in your inbox. You may want to let senders know on a permanent basis that you only look at your e-mails at certain times of the day, such as 9.30 am, 13.30 pm and 15.30 pm, and that if there is an urgent matter to give you a call. This will help manage their expectations and help you with your time/ task management. See Chapter 5 on 'Time, organizing and stress management' for more tips on using e-mails effectively to help manage your time.

Listening skills

The most important thing in communication is to hear what is being communicated both verbally and non-verbally and also to 'hear' what is not being said!

One of the important factors that can help to build relationships – and the greatest gift you can give people – is to actively listen to them. When you listen intently and focus on every word while making it clear that you are genuinely interested in what people are saying, they feel respected, their self-esteem rises and they feel more worthwhile and important. Listening actively and 'listening' non-verbally also help us to understand and deal with the differing styles of communication of men and women.

Many people are poor listeners and have never been taught how to listen properly. Almost everyone enjoys talking about themselves and it is therefore important that we practise active listening skills.

Shirley Taylor (Author, Trainer, Coach) believes that:

There are three levels of listening:

In-and-out listening, which is the lowest level. The in-and-out listener is passive or unresponsive. They are preoccupied with their own thoughts, problems and daydreams. Or they may be critically evaluating what is being said and formulating a response. Therefore, their listening phases in and out.

The next level is **literal listening**. The literal listener pays careful attention to the words being spoken, but overlooks the fact that the meaning of the message is in the *people* rather than the words themselves. By focusing on the words the literal listener often misses the *feeling* behind the words, which is a large part of the message.

Empathetic listening is the highest level of listening. The empathetic listener focuses on the complete message – the content as well as the underlying emotions, non-verbal signals, and hidden meanings. The empathetic listener is fully engaged and truly seeks to understand the speaker's point of view. They are responsive and provide feedback and encouragement to the speaker. Empathetic listening requires patience and genuine concern for the speaker.

Most people speak at an average rate of 120 words a minute. However, our brains are capable of processing more than 500 words a minute, which means that our minds start wandering off and thinking about other things and then we become poor listeners.

When you are in conversation with someone, it is appropriate to listen for at least 80 per cent of the time and speak for 20 per cent. You will speak to clarify your understanding, to show you are listening by paraphrasing, and when the other person asks you for an answer. You should also speak at the end to summarize your understanding, and you should pause before doing so as this gives you time to reflect on what you are going to say.

> "Focused listening is the ability to concentrate on every word spoken, assess what is meant by them, identify the hooks and react to them."
> (Richard Mullender, trainer and police hostage negotiator)

You can only respond to what you think you have heard and understood – make sure that you understand exactly what is being said and what is meant.

Focus on:

- choice of words;
- emphasis;
- tone of voice;
- silences/vagueness;
- repetitions;
- body language/physical condition.

If you adopt the 'listening position' your body will tell your brain that it must listen carefully. The listening position is sitting slightly forward and keeping eye contact with the speaker. People who are auditory (ie who interpret their worlds chiefly by what they hear) will automatically and involuntarily tilt their head to the side when listening.

Listen for the following:

- What exactly are they saying/meaning?
- What is not being said? (You may need to read between the lines (watch their body language) and ask questions.)
- How are they saying the words (the tone of voice)? Does it match their body language?
- What are they feeling?

- Listen for the different emotions. For example, are they anxious, worried, excited, afraid, demotivated, motivated, happy, bored or confrontational? (See Chapter 4 on 'Dealing with difficult people and managing conflict'.)

When it is appropriate to speak, you can show that you are listening by paraphrasing back to people to show that you understand, including how you think they are feeling. Empathize and reflect on the emotions they are portraying in their voice and body language, and rapport will develop.

Reflect on why they are speaking to you and what outcome they are looking for (sometimes this is not so obvious). Are they:

- giving you instructions;
- giving you feedback;
- making polite conversation and building rapport;
- asking for help;
- letting off steam;
- asking for feedback;
- looking for encouragement;
- hoping for clarification;
- trying to lay blame on someone (you, possibly)?

When listening actively you should:

- Block out all other distractions, make sure you empty your mind of everything else you need to be doing and concentrate on what the other person is saying. Listen in real time and don't be thinking about what you are going to say next, as this takes your attention away from what is being said.
- Listen with your ears, your eyes and your heart, that is, emotionally! Look for body language clues to what is really being said.
- Acknowledge verbally what you hear by saying 'hmm', 'yes', 'oh really', 'aha' etc!
- Acknowledge non-verbally what you are hearing by smiling, laughing (appropriately of course), frowning and nodding attentively now and again.
- If you are taking instructions for something then it would be expected that you make notes and ask questions (at the appropriate time) to clarify your understanding and what is expected of you.

It may be appropriate to ask permission to take notes before the conversation/meeting.

- Ask for clarification when you don't understand something the other person has said: 'Did I understand you right...?' 'Did you mean...?'

- Keep eye contact and 'listen' with your eyes.

- Be comfortable with silence – do not be afraid of pauses. Sometimes you can make a very effective statement by knowing when to say nothing!

- It is important that you show respect and don't interrupt when the other person is speaking. Otherwise, it may appear that you are only interested in getting your own point across, or that you are not interested in what they have to say, or you may stop their flow of thoughts so that they lose track of what they are trying to tell you.

- One of the most important tools of listening is simply to pause before replying, which tells people that you are thinking about what they have said, reflecting on their opinions and considering an informed reply before you answer.

- Pausing is also a good way to get other people to speak more and give you more information if you are trying to find things out.

- Summarizing what you have heard:

  - When the speaker has finished speaking, it is better to take a few seconds to think sensibly about your reply before jumping in with the first thing you can think of.

  - Pausing before you speak ensures that you avoid the risk of interrupting people if they have just stopped to gather their thoughts.

  - By carefully considering what other people have said, you are paying them a compliment. You are implicitly saying that you consider their thoughts to be important and worthy of quiet reflection, thereby making them feel worthy and important enough to be listened to, which in turn makes them feel better about themselves and helps build relationships.

  - When you summarize what has been said to prove that you have understood, you should not only summarize the content of what they said with your own words but you should also reflect the feeling of how they said it through your tone of voice (matching and pacing) and your body language (mirroring).

Active listening enables you to learn, to understand and to be able to do your job to the best of your ability. It also helps to build and maintain a high level of trust and therefore helps build relationships with your boss, your peers and your subordinates and, of course, everyone else you communicate with.

Questioning skills

The art of building relationships with your boss and your colleagues, in fact everyone you come in contact with, centres around your ability to ask questions as well as listening attentively to the answers.

You should practise the art of asking well-worded questions that focus the conversation. This helps you to understand exactly what other people are saying and feeling and it gives them an opportunity to express themselves. It means that you can find out whether your assumptions are correct or not. Asking questions is particularly important at the start of your relationship but of course it should be continued throughout your working relationship with bosses, colleagues and clients.

Different types of questions should be used to get different levels of information. Open-ended questions that are non-specific could start with the words 'Describe' or 'Tell me about'. They save you from having to ask lots of questions. These questions encourage the speaker to expand on thoughts, feelings and comments, and one question will lead to another. You can ask open-ended questions almost without limit, drawing out of the other person everything that he or she has to say. You should make a habit of asking good, open-ended questions in response to problems or difficulties. This shows interest and increases your understanding.

Open-ended questions that are specific usually begin with the 'Five Ws and H approach' – Who, What, Where, When, Why and How. These are questions designed to get the maximum amount of information and ideas, feelings and facts. An example of a neutral open question is: 'How are you feeling today?' In contrast, 'Are you happy?' is a leading question (implying happiness). Be aware that asking questions starting with 'Why' can put people on the defensive. Use closed questions to check that you have understood. These usually have a yes or no answer, and take forms such as 'Do you...?', 'Have you...?', 'Were you...?' 'Can you...?' 'Will you...?'

Probing questions are used to clarify information, to dig deeper to find out more specific information about a topic and get the details you need. However, be careful, as too many questions can sound like an interrogation!

TED will help you to remember, whenever you are given instructions, to make sure that you are entirely clear on what is needed of you. You should ask the following:

T   Tell me more about, tell me what you mean... (what is said and what is meant can be two entirely different things).

E   Explain, give Examples.

D   Describe, Details, Discuss.

Other techniques include being reflective – rephrasing what is said and returning it as a statement. Clarifying and summarizing are also valuable. Clarifying the request and asking questions (open-ended and closed-ended) will ensure that you fully understand the request. Summarizing, as already discussed, involves restating the main points of the conversation and listing any action that may need to be taken and by whom.

You should always ask questions and seek to understand so that you can deal with similar situations that arise in the future. Whenever your boss gives you an instruction and you do not understand, you must ask. Don't feel stupid about asking questions – there is only one stupid question and that is the one you don't ask. It is better to ask 10 times and get it right than not to ask and get it wrong.

Quality questions should be:

● clear;

● concise;

● need little or no clarification.

Gossip

Almost everyone gossips at some point. The most common definition of gossip is 'any conversation between two or more people about another who is not present', and if you have never been in this situation then you must be the only exception! Gossip is difficult to avoid – you have to be aware at all times as you could be dragged into gossiping innocently. Sometimes you can be empathizing with someone about someone else and this can be perceived incorrectly as gossip – remember that perception is reality for those people.

You can reduce the likelihood that any gossip will be about you or your work by remaining professional at all times. Some people who gossip enjoy disrespecting people, so you need to prevent that by not giving them any fuel to light the fire.

Gossip often has a negative connotation because discussions about people are not always based on known fact but rather on assumptions. For example, speculation about non-existent office affairs creates needless harm to the reputations of two people and causes upset and disruption that can have knock-on effects for their families.

People gossip about their company, colleagues, managers and salaries. Such talk is often based on either assumption or exaggeration, which is not helped when it is passed on from one person to another. Gossips want to know about what's going on with everyone and about work issues, and often can't wait to spread what they have learnt.

Spreading negative information about colleagues can create a lot of trouble and resentment. Any information that might damage another person should never be repeated or agreed with. You should never talk disrespect-fully about your previous employer or any past or current colleagues, as you will be perceived as being unprofessional, indiscreet, negative, a 'gossiper' and a possible trouble causer.

Assistants can act as the eyes and ears of the boss. Part of your role as an assistant is to know as much as you can about what is happening in the business and to make sure that you know everything that is going on around you within your area, your company and indeed your industry and even your competitors, so that you can make your boss aware of the key issues and develop action plans.

This does not mean that you have to act like the office spy, as people will get to realize what you are up to and distrust you. You should respect confidentiality at all times, but if there is something that will affect your boss or your organization then you should remember where your loyalties lie and use the information discreetly and appropriately.

Sometimes gossip can be useful when used in the right context and for the right reasons. It can help determine who is trustworthy, who should be avoided, and who may be able to help us accomplish our goals. Gossip can also help determine which behaviours are acceptable and which are not.

The key is to know when gossip is getting out of hand and when some-thing needs to be done about it. This might be when it is:

- hurting people's feelings;
- disrupting the flow of work;

- damaging interpersonal relationships;
- demotivating employees or damaging morale.

You can exceed your boss's expectations and offer solutions to stop the more serious type of gossiping, for example by suggesting that more communication meetings should be held, or communication should be disseminated via e-mails or voice messages to dispel any harmful rumours. It may be appropriate for your boss to speak to the culprit(s) involved to find out exactly what is happening. The person(s) involved may require coaching to change their behaviour, and in extreme circumstances it may be necessary to consider using the disciplinary procedure. Or maybe your boss needs to be more approachable, with an open-door policy so that people feel that they can talk to him or her.

If gossip is managed appropriately it need not be a problem, and there will always be the grapevine type of gossiping that can be useful in certain circumstances. So if and when gossiping does occur, be sure that you keep it professional and are sharing helpful, accurate information rather than spreading harmful rumours.

Telephone etiquette

Answer the phone with a smile on your face. The smile can be 'heard' and you will sound happy and pleasant. It takes seven seconds for a caller to realize what kind of attitude you have. If you are extremely busy and getting stressed with your work, take a deep breath before you answer the phone to calm you down and make you sound normal and not anxious.

Answer the phone promptly – don't let it ring more than three times before you answer it. Set yourself a daily challenge to attempt to answer the phone on the first ring so that callers are not kept holding for longer than necessary – they will appreciate not having their time wasted. This helps exceed expectations when you are consistent.

To help build relationships on the phone, match the caller's tone, pace and volume. As soon as they mention their name at the beginning of the call, make a note of it and use it throughout the call – people love to hear their name being used. Always be polite, helpful and proactive when dealing with phone calls. Whenever you can, go that extra mile to help the caller or client – it always pays off and sometimes how helpful you have been gets back to your boss. It improves the perception of the company and client relationships as well as your own reputation and relationships.

Always try to help callers when they ask for your boss. You will often be quite capable of dealing with the call yourself and it is amazing how many times all the caller wants is some information that you can provide. Find out as much information as possible and if appropriate make notes of the call, then inform your boss as soon as possible and get back to the caller. Callers do not always realize that you can do a lot more than just being an answering machine, so you have to ask probing questions. This also enables you to sift out the sales calls.

Understanding and communicating with different cultures

Often we can see the reason behind our own cultural ways and habits, but others may not see them in the same way. The habits, words and gestures of people from different cultures may seem odd and confusing to us. We are increasingly working across cultures and we should be aware and respectful of each other's norms and differing etiquette.

If your boss visits another country, research any cultural differences for that country to make sure that the boss does not offend anyone. The ritual of shaking hands is especially important and so too is the dress code, particularly for women. It is a good idea to provide translations of some basic greeting words – 'hello, how are you', 'thank you', 'goodbye' and so on.

When planning to do business in other countries it is advisable to try to spend a day or two in the country beforehand to do some 'on the ground' research, so, if possible, suggest this to your boss and schedule it in the diary.

Some countries take a much more direct and focused approach than others, while some will require 'small talk' and relationship building before doing business. Working with different cultures means that there will be a need for clarity in the communications we make and we should watch, listen and learn from others. However, it is worth remembering that respect, openness and courtesy are common to all cultures.

"Try to learn as much about etiquette in different cultures as possible. Find someone who is not offended if you ask questions about their culture if it is different from yours, and question away!"
(Janita C Sullivan, president, Legal Secretaries International Inc)

Be careful with the English language as it can cause confusion. The meanings of words and phrases may vary in different English-speaking countries such as the UK, Australia, South Africa and the United States.

Body language can mean different things in different countries. The common British and American 'thumbs up' (well done) gesture, for example, would be offensive in some countries. Making eye contact, showing the sole of your foot, personal space, sitting down before the other person, reading a business card, presenting an object with your left hand – all these gestures and behaviours can convey very different impressions. Be warned and watch, listen and learn.

You can find out about culture differences from the internet, from books, by asking colleagues who work in different countries and by joining cross-cultural networks such as EUMA, which also has associate organizations all over the world.

It is important to note that there is one gesture that is understood, liked and is well received by all cultures, and that is a genuine friendly smile.

Verbal and non-verbal communication, including active listening and effective questioning skills, are fundamental requirements for an assistant as they help you to grow relationships, avoid conflict and have a major impact on your effectiveness at work, including your ability to influence, persuade and negotiate.

Having the correct telephone and e-mail etiquette, as well as understanding the psychology of how people think, the different communication styles within cultures and responding in those communication styles appropriately, enables you to be an outstanding assistant. Remember, it's not just about the first impression but the long-lasting impressions and keeping up the high standards and skills expected of an exceptional assistant.

Confidence, self-belief and goal setting

If you have the right attitude and mindset you can achieve whatever you want at work and in life. This chapter will give you powerful tools and techniques to gain self-confidence, self-awareness, self-belief and self-esteem, and to set goals and self-development action plans. Gaining confidence and self-esteem is down to you, and success is about you taking action now!

"If you think you can or if you think you can't, you're right!"
(Henry Ford)

What is confidence?

Are you:

- nervous around your boss/peers;
- shy or embarrassed when you talk to people;
- able to walk into a room of strangers and start networking;
- embarrassed to give constructive criticism to colleagues and your boss;
- able to be assertive and get your point across calmly and assertively;
- afraid of presenting in public;
- afraid of organizing a large event?

Do you:

- avoid situations you do not feel comfortable with, such as the above;
- let opportunities pass you by;
- stay in your comfort zone;
- say to yourself:
    - 'I'll never be able to...'
    - 'If I had more confidence I would...'
    - 'I am not a confident type of person who can...'?

It is important to believe that confidence can be learnt in all situations!

Confidence is related to you feeling positive about yourself, a situation or an activity. It is about a way of approaching things and being in control, and although as an assistant you cannot always control what happens, you can control how you respond: that is, how you feel, think and take action. It is a belief in your own knowledge and abilities to do something in a specific situation. It is the willingness to do something, however challenging (and scary) you may feel it is.

An important feature of confidence is that it can vary at different times and in different situations; you may feel confident in one area but not in another, so you constantly need to build confidence in different fields. For example, you may be comfortable about taking minutes but not about organizing events, so that is something you may have to practise until you feel in control and confident when organizing any type of event.

The feeling of confidence

Understand what your body does when it feels confident and 'anchor' the feeling of self-confidence.

Think about a time when you were confident, and remember and fully visualize the feelings you had at that time. If you are feeling and thinking confidently, your body takes on a 'confidence stance' that is unique to you. It could be standing tall with head high, shoulders back, breathing from your abdomen and legs strong, with arms slightly away from your body and palms facing outwards. Your mind believes your own body language, and if you take on what is a confident stance for you then your brain believes that you are actually feeling confident. If you act confident or if you fake confidence, then you become confident.

Each time you want to feel confident, go back into your confidence stance and it will automatically bring positive feelings into your conscious mind.

The opposite of this is that if you are slumped in your chair with your head hanging down and your body leaning to one side, and with your breathing high in your chest, there is no way that your mind will believe that at that moment you are feeling confident. When you have found what your non-confident state is, recognize it and avoid it.

Use the confidence stance whenever you need to feel confident, especially if you are just about to enter a room for an appraisal, an important meeting or an interview and the like.

Act as if you are confident

You will see people all the time who look confident because of the way they walk and talk, their attitude, the way they dress, sit, stand and deal with other people. Start to put in place some of the traits that you see in them. Find out what confident-looking people think in certain situations by asking them. What goes through their head in the situations where they might feel anxious or nervous that helps them to deal with those things?

Think positive thoughts

Choose positive thoughts, because what you think influences your actions, your actions affect your results, and results affect your confidence. In any situation you should think about whether the way you think is helping or hindering you, and if it is hindering you then change the way you think.

Focus on your strengths and boost your confidence

Help to build self-confidence by focusing on your strengths, improving on any weaknesses and learning to like yourself. Think about the things that you like about yourself, including your skills, knowledge, behaviours and personality traits. Consider what has brought you success so far. Remind yourself of all the challenges that you have faced and overcome.

As a way of realizing what your talents are and to start boosting your self-confidence, just take a moment to write down your talents. These may relate to home and/or work life.

My talents are:
(supervisory, loyalty, organizational skills, supportive, able to adapt to change easily, innovative, keeping confidences, etc)

1

2

3

I use these talents when I:
(look after my boss, help other secretaries, present to a group, help friends, teach my children, etc)

1

2

3

I could use my talents more by:
(exceeding expectations, using them on my children, in my home life, raising money for charity and putting something back into the community, etc)

1

2

3

Remind yourself of how great you are on a regular basis, particularly during times when you feel your confidence needs a boost. When you go to bed at night, think about what went well that day and what you have achieved. Write down all the things that you have done successfully, adding to the list as you achieve more. Use the list to boost your confidence when you feel you need it. You will begin to notice how good you really are and your confidence will grow.

Confidence brings the ability to 'speak out' in many different ways and circumstances. You will feel you can take on new challenges in different situations. You will also notice changes in your body language, with movements and posture appearing more self-assured.

Self-esteem, self-awareness and self-belief

Our beliefs have a strong effect on our self-esteem, which is the 'picture' of ourselves that we carry around in our minds. Self-esteem is to do with identity, feelings of self-worth, and values and relationships with others. If we receive positive messages, we are likely to have higher self-esteem, and it therefore follows that if we receive negative messages, whether true or not, we will develop low self-esteem.

Those with low self-esteem react to change negatively, suffering anxiety and stress, believing that they are unlucky and wondering why bad things are always happening to them. Those with high self-esteem will welcome change and see it as an opportunity to enhance their lives and an exciting challenge to take on.

High self-esteem increases self-assurance, happiness and well-being and is the key to successful achievement, contentment and happiness. In order to increase our self-esteem we have to become self-aware and believe in ourselves.

The subconscious mind comes into play here. When we are good at something we excel in it and confidence flows. When we think we are not good at something then we just don't do it well.

Conscious and subconscious minds

We have approximately 70,000 thoughts each day that determine what we think, what we feel, what we say, how we react, what habits we establish and how ultimately we are perceived. These are just our conscious thoughts; we have seven times as many thoughts going on in our subconscious mind that we are unaware of until something pops into our consciousness.

An example of subconscious thought is when we drive a car: how often have you driven somewhere and realized that you never even thought about how to get there – you just arrived? You did not have to think about changing gear or indicating or looking in your mirror; you have been driving for so long that you do it automatically and without having to think about it.

The subconscious mind 'covers' about 88 per cent of your mind, while the other 12 per cent is covered by the conscious mind. The subconscious part is responsible for storing your memory, habits, personality, self-image and beliefs. It also controls bodily functions.

The conscious mind is the leader and tells our subconscious mind how to react. The conscious mind leads, loves and protects while the subconscious follows, respects and trusts.

> You can tell your subconscious mind anything and it believes you – it cannot tell the difference between reality and imagination. Changing the negative things you think by replacing them with positive thoughts gives you the power to tap into the power of your subconscious mind. Convince yourself you are the best and you will become the best.

Internal 'negative gremlins' and internal 'positive coach'

The most important person you'll ever talk and listen to is yourself. You can encourage yourself and be positive or you can criticize yourself, sometimes unnecessarily, and become negative. Constructive criticism is always good to listen to, whether it comes from yourself or someone else. I call the inner voice that criticizes you destructively the 'negative gremlin'.

The negative gremlin is the persistent voice deep inside your subconscious mind that:

- makes you feel guilty about something;
- points out your faults, which are sometimes untrue;
- tells you that you can't do 'this' or 'that';
- overlooks your strengths and good points;
- can make you feel powerless to change;
- when you have a setback, says 'I told you so', 'I knew that would happen';
- reminds you of your weak points and previous failures;
- reinforces what other people may have told you in the past (which may not be true or be attempts to 'put you down' as sometimes jealousy may cause people to tell lies about you).

Parents tell children to be careful because they want to keep them safe. However, subconsciously this makes children worry about things and embeds fears into their subconscious minds. These can become limiting beliefs that can actually harm their self-confidence in later years at work and prevent them from succeeding and from taking calculated risks. We should encourage our children to challenge their fears, not reiterate them. Parents also tend to tell their children not to show off and that they should be modest. When they do this they are stopping young people from expressing themselves and from being creative. This can stifle their true personalities, which in turn affects the way they react when they grow up.

Our past experiences can influence our ability to handle the present. In order to change the way we think about ourselves and be able to increase our confidence and self-esteem, we need to bring these limiting self-beliefs into our conscious mind and work on making them into positive thoughts and positive beliefs about ourselves. Once you start to change your thoughts, your actions and reactions will change, and so will the way you are perceived.

The voice that we should listen to is our inner 'positive coach'. The positive coach is the voice that:

- looks at things with a positive frame of mind and dispels negativity;

- encourages you to improve;

- accepts you the way you are;

- encourages you to accept a challenge and enjoy it – 'you'll feel good when you've done it';

- helps you to learn from mistakes and think about what you can do differently next time;

- helps you to get rid of the negative gremlins and focus on the future rather than be stuck in the past where you still acknowledge negative belief systems and habits.

Try to encourage the voice of the positive coach to talk to you more and dispel the negative gremlins. Then you will have a sunnier outlook on life, you will enjoy your work and you will have self-esteem, self-belief and confidence.

The following are empowering questions to ask yourself in order to change the negative gremlins into positive actions:

- How can I turn this weakness into a strength – what steps do I need to take?

- How can I turn this problem into an opportunity?

- Who do I need to be to achieve my dream? Who could be my mentor?

● If I imagine what I would be like in one or two years' time and look back, what lessons would I have learnt? What steps would I have taken to get there? (This is a technique called timeline, used in NLP.)

> Focus on what you want and will do and not on what you don't want and won't do. Research on thought suppression has shown that trying to avoid a thought makes it even more active in your mind (eg if I say 'Don't think about a blue elephant!' – what are you seeing in your mind's eye?). The same holds true when it comes to behaviour (eg if I say 'Don't turn round now and look at the lady behind you' – what do you immediately do?)

Fear

Many of us have a fear of something – of rejection, of stepping out of our comfort zone, of failure, of being laughed at, of change, of taking risks, of not fitting in, of 'going blank' (especially when giving presentations), of not being worthy and so on.

FEAR stands for:

False

Expectations

Appearing

Real.

Ninety per cent of our fears are not real. They are 'what if' situations where we worry and nothing comes of it.

Think back to how many times you have been worried about something that never happened and how many times you had False Expectations Appearing Real. They lie deep in our subconscious and you will be able to get rid of them. Next time you feel FEAR and are worrying about something, think logically about it and reframe your beliefs: in other words, think about it in a different and positive way that makes the negative feelings disappear. You need a clear vision, a strong will and energy so that you can ignore the knock-backs and reach your goals.

List your limiting beliefs, and ask yourself: What are these beliefs doing for me? How are they stopping me from moving forward and being the person I want to be? What beliefs would I rather have? By discarding limiting beliefs for enabling ones we become empowered.

One way to build self-confidence is to face our fears and prove to ourselves that indeed we can do it. This is getting out of our comfort zone. The more we practise something, the better we become at it; and the better we feel about it, the more confident we become. Then it sits within our comfort zone and we feel confident.

> The secret of confidence and self-belief is not to dwell on what has gone before and what has gone wrong in your life, but to focus on where you want to go and what you want to do – and to really believe you will get there.

When your mind tells you something many times, your heart will follow. If you want to persuade yourself that something you want can be accomplished, keep saying it to yourself and something great will happen – just by thinking positively. It works the same way if you voice something negative time after time, so be careful about what you say and think!

Tools to change/eliminate negative gremlin voices

These must be practised over and over before they become automatic.

Mickey Mouse voice

Bill Docherty MBE, a master practitioner in NLP, says that an effective way of getting rid of negative gremlins and limiting voices that lurk in your conscious mind is to imagine the voices to be like a 'Mickey Mouse' high-pitched squeak (which you should not and cannot take seriously). If you want, you can speed the voice up, make it even squeakier and imagine throwing it away – subconsciously your mind will not allow your conscious mind to listen to it any more because it sounds just too silly!

Another technique is just to laugh at the negative gremlin and its limiting belief – don't believe anything it says and treat it as a joke.

Affirmations

You can convince your subconscious mind that you are going to succeed by repeating your goal or your positive belief over and over again. Soon your subconscious will be telling you in your sleep that you're going to succeed. Tell yourself that you can do something, and then keep at it until you do it. This technique requires tenacity!

Positive affirmations are the opposite of the deep-seated negative beliefs that rest in your subconscious. You have to consciously tell yourself whatever it is that you want to feel good at or about, and then it will eventually become part of your subconscious. Positive affirmations will help rid you of the negative gremlins. You have to say the positive affirmations in the present tense and not in the future tense, which would give your brain an excuse to put it off when actually you need to start believing it now. You should use a powerful tone, stressing the positivity and using words that make you feel good. You need to say them every day until you can re-programme your brain to make it feel optimistic and positive, giving you confidence and self-esteem which in turn motivate a 'can do' and 'will do' attitude.

Affirmations will work best if you can think of the positive outcomes and benefits of believing them. Think about how affirmations will affect the way you are perceived by others, how it will make you feel when it works. For example, when you hear 'I'm not good enough to...' say 'I **am** good enough to...'.

You could write your affirmations on Post-it notes and stick them to your fridge at home, or on your mirror so that you see them every morning and every night when you brush your teeth. You could put them somewhere in your office (but not around your screen as this is ergonomically incorrect and can make your desk look untidy). If you are a 'visual' person then you could make them different colours or different types of writing and draw pictures around them.

If you are an 'auditory' person you could record your affirmations and listen to them before you get up in the morning and/or before you go to sleep or while driving in your car, or say them out loud when you read them in your book or from your Post-it notes. If you prefer, you could even sing them!

If you are a 'kinaesthetic' person, write down your feelings as well as your affirmation.

Keep on reviewing and eliminating negative gremlins until you are full of confidence and self-esteem, and ready to take on the office if not the world.

Suggested affirmation: 'Limiting beliefs no longer rule me – I rule my limiting beliefs and everything is possible!'

In order for you to be able to do things, you have to believe that you can do them, trust yourself and believe in yourself and your abilities. Your own thoughts manifest themselves into your own reality.

Noticing and rephrasing

You have to be aware when the negative gremlin starts to rise and notice that it is starting to talk so that you can do something about it. Sometimes this can manifest itself in physical symptoms such as shallow breathing, a furrowed brow, holding your breath, tension headaches, stomach ulcers and even – in extreme cases – heart attacks. Sometimes you may just notice thoughts that flit into your mind every day: the ones where you put yourself down, such as 'I've lost that telephone number I promised to give to my boss – I'm stupid!', 'Why did I forget to organize a visa for my boss's visit to China? I'm pathetic!' We all do it: we call ourselves names. Well, now you will stop doing that because you will notice yourself doing it. You can tell yourself: 'Everyone makes mistakes; I'll learn from this and I will not let it happen again.' Your positive coach should come into play and be more encouraging, positive and supportive, helping you to come up with solutions to any problems.

You should take deep breaths to get the oxygen circulating in your body, and you should repeat your affirmation(s).

When you start to listen to your negative gremlin, try to reframe it and ask yourself what your positive coach would say to the gremlin right now. Keep on doing it until it becomes a habit to have the positive coach speaking to you all the time.

Sometimes you hear your negative gremlin saying things like 'I can't do that,' 'I can't tell the boss how I feel,' 'I can't work that machine,' 'I can't learn a new system,' 'I can't learn a new language,' 'I can't ask for a pay rise,' 'I can't...', 'I can't...', 'I can't'. When that happens, you should change the word 'can't' to 'won't' or 'I choose not to', because you can do anything you put your mind to but you may choose not to do it.

When you hear your negative gremlin talking about 'I must...', 'I should...', 'I ought to...', you may start to feel anxious as this is something that you feel you have to do and you may not want or really need to do it. In contrast, the positive coach would give you the choice of whether you will or you won't do something. When you choose you have freedom – the freedom of choice – and therefore less anxiety. Once you have made a decision – whether you choose to do something or you choose not to do something – that also relieves stress and anxiety and gets rid of negative gremlins. If you decide you will do something but will do it later, then make sure that it is on your 'to do' list so you don't forget. Once you have written it down, the negative gremlin will stop bothering you and will let you get on with your work.

Also, change the word 'need' to 'want'. Ask yourself the question: 'Do I really need...?' In work you may need a break but not take one because you feel you don't have time. If you say 'I want a break,' it makes you think that you are allowed a break and you can take one and come back refreshed and energized.

The law of attraction

The law of attraction says that whatever we expect becomes a self-fulfilling prophecy. When we confidently expect to succeed or learn something from every experience and believe that good things will happen, they will. When we expect a negative outcome to a situation, then the outcome will usually be negative.

What we expect plays a key role in what we attract and in our outcomes, and also has a remarkable effect on the people around us. What we expect from those around us determines our attitude towards them. In turn, the people around us tend to reflect our attitudes back at us – whether the expectations and attitudes are positive or negative, good or bad. A positive, optimistic, cheerful attitude will cause people to want to help you, and will cause things to happen the way you want them to happen.

Therefore look for the good in every situation. Look for the valuable lesson in every setback or difficulty. Be positive and cheerful about every-thing that happens and you will be amazed at the difference it makes in your life.

Your entire life is an expression of your thinking. If you improve the quality of your thinking, you will inevitably improve the quality of your life.

"The most powerful law in the universe is the 'law of attraction' – you have the ability to transform any weakness or suffering into strength, power, perfect peace, health and abundance. If you think positively, you will attract positive vibes. In whatever you do, make excellence your standard. Belief determines actions and actions determine results, but first you have to believe."
(Narisa B Espinoza – 2012 president, Philippine Association of Secretaries & Administrative Professionals, Inc – Cebu Chapter)

Take ownership of your own personal development – nobody is going to do it for you. If you need to develop your skills more, find out how and do it. A definition of confidence is: 'belief in yourself and your abilities'.

The power of experiential learning

Plan your learning: develop confidence through learning and doing. Once you know the areas in which you wish to be more confident, you can begin to identify actions you can take to help you achieve this. Confident people are only confident because they have learnt the skills or knowledge that they need or want.

Most people are capable of far more than they admit to themselves. Overcoming this self-doubt can simply be a matter of creating safe opportunities to practise and, by experiencing success, increase their confidence in their abilities.

The power of experiential learning is extremely valuable. To become more confident, we have to do something. Belonging to a group like EUMA lends itself extremely well in this respect as members can practise and experiment with all kinds of different skills and behaviours – such as chairing meetings, organizing events and presenting to a group in a safe environment – before they take them back into their work environment as confident practitioners.

Continual learning

> "One of my bosses did not see the value of sending assistants to professional seminars and conferences. I did not stop asking him every year – and finally he gave in. Later on, I found out what I should have replied to his frequent question: 'What if I train you and you leave?' Of course I should have said: 'What if you don't train me and I stay!'"
> (Heli Puputti, past European chairman for EUMA)

Each and every one of us needs to continually learn and develop if we want to be at the top of our game, lead fulfilling exciting lives, have the knowledge to teach our children, be successful and reach our goals. If we don't learn something new, then: 'If you always do what you've always done, you'll always get what you always got' (W L Bateman).

There is also a saying: 'You learn something new every day.' This is especially true if you open yourself up to opportunities such as project work.

Imagine what you can achieve by actively seeking out your own learning and development. Wanting to continually self-develop says something about your personality, professionalism, self-worth and drive. For all of us it means that we become more effective and more interesting as we learn. What is most evident is that people who are willing to learn are the most successful.

Assistants need to keep up with the latest technology, computer programs, social media and electronic gadgets that affect our daily living. Some bosses may need dragging and kicking into using them but they'll thank you in the end. Learning is a necessary work and life skill!

Continual development is about feeling the fear and facing it anyway, taking yourself out of your comfort zone, learning new skills and behaviours, and gaining knowledge. Do something you haven't done before that will stretch you and increase your skills and abilities and leave you feeling exhilarated. It could be organizing a secretarial communication meeting, chairing it and possibly presenting at it. It could be taking on a project for your boss or your organization. It could be attending networking events and meeting new people.

> *"To become a successful assistant you need to be interested in everything that is going on around you, and to constantly try to learn and understand what the other responsibilities are. Continuous development/learning is the best way to be successful and you should not be afraid to get involved with project work even if it is outside your remit."*
>
> (Brigitte Thethy)

> *"The skills I learned as a PA proved to be invaluable. I can't think of any other profession where I would have learned the skills to transition into being the editor of a newspaper."*
>
> (Christine Davies (ex-PA), editor-in-chief, *The Bodrum Observer*, one of the founders of EUMA)

You are in charge of your ongoing self-development and you should take the responsibility for making it happen. You are in charge of motivating yourself to unlock your potential to maximize your performance! Everything you learn will benefit you, your boss, your organization, your family and your life as a whole, and there are many ways to continually find ways to develop yourself.

Methods of learning

- Attending conferences/seminars, webinars and virtual conferences;
- internet surfing;
- on-the-job development (eg secondment, project work, job shadowing, involvement in a focus group);
- practising new skills (eg chairing meetings);
- taking yourself out of your comfort zone (eg giving presentations);
- mentor/coach;
- reading a self-help book like this one (so pat yourself on your back for buying it and enjoy!);
- research and reading – internal and external publications, newsletters, articles;
- self-help videos, DVD, CDs;
- e-learning (computer-based training);
- studying for a professional qualification part time at university etc;
- networking (eg EUMA, **www.euma.org**);
- instructor-led programmes – participating in courses, workshops, seminars, briefings;
- internal courses;
- appraisals/feedback;
- learning from mistakes (treat them as a learning curve and know that you are allowed to make mistakes – you are after all only human; don't agonize over any mistakes you've made – just learn from them and don't repeat them);
- teaching others – motivates us to learn more;
- asking questions and listening to people with proven track records in the area in which you want to be successful.

Appraisals and feedback

You should always ask for feedback and welcome constructive criticism, because we all see ourselves in a certain way and as doing certain things, but other people perceive us differently. It is useful to have feedback from others, to take their comments on board, think seriously about them and do something about them.

Appraisals are the best time to have this discussion but you should ask for feedback at any time, especially if you have just completed a project and would like to know how it had been received. This can lead to good news or constructive feedback to help with your self-development.

When you have your appraisal there is a golden rule that nothing should be a surprise. That means you should have been receiving continuous feedback. Especially if something has not gone so well, there should have been feedback at the time it happened.

Most people do not have regular feedback processes, either because they do not realize how important it is, or because they are uncomfortable giving and receiving feedback. By missing opportunities to share necessary information, team members are prevented from capitalizing on their strengths and identifying areas for improvement.

Feedback is important for the following reasons:

- People want to do a good job.
- Without feedback, it is impossible for people to learn how to be more effective.
- Constructive, non-judgemental feedback is both instructive and empowering.

Ask for feedback if it is not forthcoming, and let the person know what you plan to do with it. If people see you using their feedback as a stimulus to try doing things differently, they are likely to give you more.

Tips on how to receive constructive criticism

For an appraisal meeting the room should be set out so that the two chairs are not separated by a table and are at 45° angles to each other. As mentioned earlier, this reduces any psychological barriers and encourages a successful meeting.

Accepting feedback in the form of either good news or constructive criticism is an important learning experience. First, you have to accept and believe that constructive criticism is necessary for you to be successful. Feedback is someone else's opinion, so you are allowed to accept or reject it as long as you have good reason.

Allow the appraiser to complete what he or she is saying; wait at least three seconds before responding as opposed to reacting. Keep your emotions under control and stay calm. Try not to take criticism as a personal attack; it is about your work, not you, and it is about improving your performance.

If people have given you constructive criticism, it should be backed up with examples/proof and not just reflect subjective feelings. If they have not given any examples then ask for them. If they have not got any and you disagree with the feedback, then say so. Follow the rules on being assertive that you will find in Chapter 4 on 'Dealing with difficult people and managing conflict'.

Finally, thank the person for the feedback. It is up to you whether you choose to act on it, consider it or simply ignore it. If you wish to act on it, then you can update your goals and your personal development plan.

Remember that life is not a dress rehearsal. When opportunities to learn arise, seize the moment and increase your skills. This is your opportunity to take ownership of your own destiny.

Personal development plan (PDP)

Appendix 2 is a PDP which can be downloaded online (see front of book for details).

You should be clear about your own PDP, knowing what activities you intend to undertake and how you are going to make these happen and when. You should look out for opportunities to put them into practice and work with your boss to make them happen. When opportunities arise – grasp them with both hands.

A PDP will let you understand yourself better and help you commit to and focus on your personal development/learning and training requirements. It will enable you to identify gaps in your skills and experience and find ways to fill those gaps. You will reflect on past experiences and focus on learning outcomes; the end product will be that your self-confidence will be boosted and you will have a satisfying and successful career. You can use this PDP in your appraisal meetings and to help you in career management.

The PDP helps you to recognize any opportunities that you can take advantage of, as well as any threats that you need to be aware of and mitigate or eliminate. Once you complete it, your motivation and self-esteem will grow through achieving your objectives and goals.

It can be for your eyes (and thought processes) only, or you can share the information with your boss in your appraisal meetings or when you are looking for a pay rise or promotion. It can also help you to put your curriculum vitae together. PDPs can also be linked into the way you add value to your organization.

Regular reviews of the PDP are essential to ensure that you are on track and it is still relevant. Schedule six-monthly reviews of your PDP in your diary and keep it relevant and up to date. It could be built into your formal appraisal system.

Remember to reward yourself when goals and objectives are met.

Goal setting

 You need to set goals because: 'If you're not sure where you're going, you'll probably end up somewhere else.'

What are the goals that, on your deathbed, you will either be glad you achieved or regret not having achieved?

Goal setting will help:

- build relationships at work when you align your goals with those of your boss and the organization;
- build your self-confidence as you achieve your goals;
- motivate you;
- separate what is important from what is irrelevant;
- understand what is important for you to achieve;
- make you satisfied with your life when you are sat in your rocking chair at the age of 99!

When you set goals, you have to *want* to achieve them, and the reason for that has to be stressed strongly to ensure that you will achieve them. You don't have to hit all your goals at once, but start with the ones that matter to you most and will make the biggest difference once you achieve them.

Appendix 4 has a pro forma for goal-setting that you can use to set your goals; this can also be downloaded online (see front of book for details).

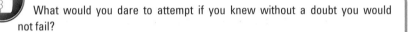

What would you dare to attempt if you knew without a doubt you would not fail?

Without a doubt the worst behaviour is avoidance – thinking we cannot achieve a goal and not even trying because we are afraid of failing. Aim high and believe you have the ability to reach your goals and believe you have the ability to improve. Embracing the fact that you **can** change and improve will allow you to make better choices and reach your fullest potential. It's the actions you take that help you achieve your goals that make you successful. Always give 100 per cent and aim for 100 per cent – forgive yourself if you don't reach there the first time, but try again. Be tenacious and willing to commit to long-term goals and be persistent in the face of difficulty.

You should learn to recognize and seize opportunities that present themselves to help you achieve your goals. We often fail to notice the opportunities simply because of how busy we are and how many goals we juggle at once. Decide when and where you will take action in advance, as planning will help your brain detect and seize any opportunities that might arise, which increases your chance of success greatly.

When you set yourself a goal, be as specific and precise as possible to give yourself a clear idea of what success looks like. Knowing exactly what you want to achieve keeps you motivated until you get there, leaving no room for doubt about what you need to do, and whether or not you have actually done it.

To help you successfully reach your goals, you should build your will-power and self-control by exercising them; for example, take on a challenge that requires you to get out of your comfort zone and learn a new skill. When you find yourself wanting to give in, do one step at a time and make a plan for how you will deal with troubles when they occur. It may be hard in the beginning, but it will get easier. As your strength grows and you succeed in reaching your goals, you can take on more to keep exercising your will-power.

Word of caution: Be a realistic optimist when you are setting goals, be positive about achieving them and believe in your ability to succeed but don't underestimate how difficult it can be to reach your goal. Most goals worth achieving require time, planning, effort and persistence.

Steps to help you achieve your goals

- Make sure you read over the completed goal sheet several times a week and dream/imagine living the goal several times a week or even every day.

- Close your eyes, relax, smile, and see your goal as though it were already a reality.

- Visualizing the end result helps you act and feel as if you have already achieved your goal.

- Base your goals firmly on your values.

- Write or type them – don't just have them in your head. Make them 'SMARTER' – see Appendix 4.

- Put some fun into your goals and enjoy the activity.

- If it is appropriate, you can share your goals with others. Work-related ones in particular should be shared with your boss.

- Align your goals and objectives with those of your boss and your organization.

- Evaluate your goals and revise them regularly as things change, including yourself. If you don't know how well you are doing, you can't adjust your behaviour or strategies accordingly.

- Write the goals in the present tense and word them positively, because if you write 'I will do whatever...' this does not tell the subconscious mind to start working today. It will put things off until tomorrow and we all know tomorrow never comes.

- Reward yourself along the way when you achieve your mini goals – it is what keeps you going when things get tough.

- make sure you really want the goal to enable you to achieve success.

- Sign your goal-setting form – that makes it a binding contract (subconsciously it will make you achieve it).

- Set priorities. When you have several goals, give each a priority and do not have too many at the same time. This helps you to avoid feeling overwhelmed by too many goals, and helps to direct your attention to the most important ones.

- You should set goals over which you have as much control as possible. It is disheartening if you do not achieve a personal goal for reasons beyond your control.

Once you have achieved a goal:

- Take the time to enjoy the satisfaction and implications of achieving the goal.

- Reward yourself when you achieve goals and even when you achieve milestones in the goals you set. All of this helps you build the self-confidence you deserve.

- Evaluate how easily you achieved the goal. If you conclude that your goals are set too low or are not challenging enough, then set harder and more challenging ones that will increase your self-confidence and self-belief.

- Learn from achieving the goal – assess what went well and what didn't go so well, and evaluate and revise your other goals accordingly. Write the findings in your PDP.

- Even though you achieved the goal, you may have realized that there is a skill gap or that you might need some experience in a certain area. If so, set another goal to achieve this.

- If you fail to achieve a goal, look at whether you need to set slightly easier goals so that they are achievable. Learn from the outcome.

You only have one life – work at it, accomplish what you want to and enjoy it!

Look back at this chapter and consider the actions you might take to build your self-confidence. Write down your answers and transfer some of them immediately into goals or onto your PDP, which can be found in Appendix 2 and can be downloaded online.

1 What goals do you want to define with regard to building self-confidence? It can be useful to think about your levels of confidence on a scale of 1 to 10 (1 being low and 10 being high). Define the level your confidence is at now and the level you want in the future. Remember that you may have to think of different situations and score yourself for each situation, because when you are outside your comfort zone you are likely to be less confident.

2 How could you develop the skills or knowledge you have identified? For each goal, make a list of all the possible actions you can take to help increase your confidence. This means that you will be starting to build some detail into your PDP.

3 What would be really helpful for you to say to yourself to make you feel more confident and have more self-belief?

4 Who could you involve to inspire or help you?

5 In what areas do you want to improve?

6 What can you learn from your past experiences? Ask yourself the following questions on a regular basis to help you to build your confidence and self-esteem:
   – What went well? It's important to understand the positives to build your self-esteem and confidence.
   – What did not go so well? Learn from these mistakes to set goals and improve. Think about what you can do differently next time.

7 What skills or knowledge would be really good for you to learn to help you be more confident?

Develop an attitude of unshakable confidence in yourself and your ability to reach your goals. This chapter is about building your 'self-awareness', 'self-confidence' and 'self-belief'. You should now be absolutely convinced that nothing can stop you from achieving what you set out to achieve and to be motivated to continually learn and improve.

Dealing with difficult people and managing conflict

04

When people are asked why they left their last job, the answer often involves a difficult boss. Some are really bad and no one finds it easy to work with them, while others simply have some very annoying habits. Sometimes an employee and a boss have a personality clash. If you do consider you have a difficult boss, you should try to find out whether the problem lies with you, your boss, or a combination of the two.

Think about whether you seem to have more problems with your boss than your colleagues do. If so, maybe your work styles do not match. If everyone finds this manager challenging, then you are most likely working for someone difficult.

Often the way people treat us says more about them than it does about us. Think about what lies behind their thoughts and actions. Do they chase, bully, react the way they do because they are feeling out of control or inadequate and insecure themselves? Are they being bullied and under pressure from their own boss or clients? Try to empathize with their situation.

While some people may handle disagreements better than others, our natural reaction to conflict is the fight-or-flight reflex. In a conflict situation, the fight reaction can translate into confronting, arguing, yelling, and even shoving or hitting. At the other end of the continuum, the flight reaction causes us to quickly give in to others, leave uncomfortable situations or avoid bringing up difficult issues. Neither fight nor flight behaviours are likely to result in solving the problem that's causing the conflict. Using the strategies and tips in this chapter can help you move from conflict to problem resolution.

A problem-solving technique

Appendix 5 provides a problem-solving technique that helps you to be objective and systematic when solving any problem or conflict; it is easy to follow and self-explanatory. You can download the problem-solving master form online (see front of book for details) and use it as many times as you need to. Remember to evaluate the solution and the outcome, and revisit the problem if necessary.

Nearly all of us, at some time in our working lives, have to deal with difficult situations and difficult people. We therefore need to learn how to manage conflict to make sure that we continue enjoying going to work and building effective and efficient working relationships. Conflict can at best cause unproductive work days, and often leads to stress-related problems that result in sickness and absence from work. There is even a possibility of it ending in your losing or resigning from your job. According to the 2011 UK Chartered Management of Personnel and Development (CIPD) *Absence Management* survey report, management styles are the number-two cause of stress at work (number one being the volume of work given by management). Conflict is likely to be due to one or a combination of the following reasons:

- bad communication;
- personality clashes;
- conflicting interests;
- jealousy;
- competition;
- personal agendas;
- deadlines and time constraints;
- aggressive personalities;
- having different immediate goals (needs), or different values and things that are important to us;
- having a different approach to situations (eg work styles);
- incorrect perception of situations and people.

Bear in mind that what one party perceives as conflict may not be seen as such by the other party. Remember too that some people may seem 'difficult' because of the way we interact with them. We may have created the difficulty in the first place, or they may have personality issues and difficult characteristics.

Conflict most often occurs when the needs of both parties are not being met in some way, so it may be that you have to arrive at a compromise as, in the words of Napoleon Hill: 'There are three sides to most disagreements: your side, the other person's side, and the right side... which is probably somewhere in the middle.' The most efficient and effective way to agree on the 'middle' is by being assertive.

Assertiveness

Assertiveness is a strategy for gaining mutual respect that helps resolve conflicts. It is the key to good, clear, professional communication. It is about being neither passive and walked all over nor aggressive and confrontational – it's about getting your point across in a confident manner. When you use assertiveness you can negotiate changes by stating directly what you think, feel and want.

Think about the way you are perceived by others, which includes the way you sound, the words you use and how your attitudes affect other people. Being assertive means that you take responsibility for your own wants, needs and decisions. It results in better working relationships and less stress, as feelings of guilt and anger won't build up and it will save time and energy.

People who are not assertive will often give up easily and the assertive ones will stand up for their 'rights'. As long as they are being reasonable, they should be tenacious and persistent in order to enforce their beliefs and achieve a win–win outcome.

An assistant will constantly need to demonstrate assertiveness in his or her role with both the boss and colleagues. However, it is not appropriate to be assertive in every situation. The choice of strategy will depend on your own short- and long-term goals and those of the other people involved. You need to anticipate their likely response to your chosen strategy and the implications of the possible outcome.

Being assertive will enable you to express your feelings, ideas, wishes, suggestions, needs, opinions and rights directly and honestly without the other person getting angry, anxious, upset or defensive, while respecting the feelings, attitudes, wishes, opinions and rights of others. This may include expressing such emotions as empathy, anger, fear, caring, hope, joy, despair, indignation or embarrassment, and these will be expressed in a manner that does not violate other people's rights.

> When you have a conflict situation, ignoring the problem is not an option. You should aim for a win–win outcome by using assertiveness to get your point across without being overbearing and abusing other people's rights. It is about self-respect and respect for others.

Figure 4.1 sets out a simple strategy for being assertive in order to solve problems and avoid conflict.

FIGURE 4.1 Assertiveness/problem solving/conflict management

State confidently, clearly and succinctly what the situation/problem is and 'listen' to understand

(50% of all problems can be sorted at this point)

(Use a private neutral room to meet)

'I feel...', 'I need...'
(Remember to use 'I' statements)

What do you need? How do you feel? (Submissive people need you to ask them what they want)

State confidently, calmly, specifically, giving examples if appropriate, adult to adult

My rights   **Your rights**

Listen/question and empathize

Be flexible/compromise/ negotiate – how do we resolve this situation?

Solution

Focus on the future not the past
Focus on the solution not the problem

Win–win outcome

Remember: Assertiveness is about self-respect and respect for others

Say what you feel

If you let things build up and you don't express your feelings and needs, you will eventually feel resentment. Your reactions and body language may confuse people as they are not mind readers and may not understand your point of view. If you feel yourself getting angry, then say something for everyone's sake.

If you practise being assertive you are less likely to be exploited, professionally and personally. You are more likely to be successful in your career and you will be seen as a more competent and confident person.

It is important to understand the difference between assertion and aggression. Assertion becomes aggression when it involves destructive behaviour and when you start to undermine others, inciting colleagues against the people you are in conflict with, trying to damage their reputations in order to reduce their status or to get revenge. Insulting people is also aggressive behaviour and should be avoided at all costs.

Learn to say 'no' to requests when you need to

You need to set boundaries, let other people know what these are and believe that there are times when it is right to say no.

When a request is made of you and you cannot oblige on this occasion, there are three ways of saying 'No':

- *The 'direct No'*: No, I can't and the reason for that is...

- *The 'soft No'*: I understand your needs and understand how important it is. On this occasion I cannot do what you want, but what I can do is find a solution – perhaps find someone else to do it for you, or maybe you could type it up in draft yourself and I will format it tomorrow.

- *The 'pre-emptive No'*: Where you know someone is going to ask you 'Are you able to do...?' Before they start you say: 'I am so looking forward to getting away on time tonight as I have to go to...' Then they either won't ask or will understand better when you say no!

Remember – you are only refusing a request, not rejecting a person. State your own position clearly and confidently. Look for a solution and offer a compromise: 'I can't work late this evening, but as it is important I'm prepared to come in early tomorrow.' Or: 'I can't work late this evening, but as it is important I will ask my colleague to stay for you on this occasion and I will do the same for him or her when I can.'

Conflict can be destructive when it results in frustration, confusion, divided teams, low morale and demotivated staff. However, it can also be constructive when it opens up discussions, promotes creativity and solutions, clarifies issues and results in higher performance.

Dealing with sarcasm

If you're the victim of sarcasm, don't ignore it or pretend it didn't happen – deal with it assertively. Once the individual has given their sarcastic comment, look at them, pause, then repeat what they said word for word and pause again, leaving the comment hanging in the air for them to explain.

Sarcastic people tend to defend their use of sarcasm by protesting that they were joking or that you do not have a sense of humour. Do not react. Instead say, 'If you have a concern about... I am happy to talk with you about it.' They will soon come to realize that you are not a passive victim. Instead of using sarcasm to make people laugh, cultivate humour that doesn't require a victim.

> *"Humour is a rubber sword – it allows you to make a point without drawing blood."*
>
> (Mary Hirsh)

Sometimes it may be your behaviour that perpetuates or exasperates a conflict further

You should arrange a meeting with the person you have a conflict with and state that you would like to explain your behaviour and how you feel and to talk about how they feel. Explain to them that when they do... it irritates you because... and it makes you feel... and therefore you withdraw yourself and tend not to speak unless you have to. Encourage them to let you know if anything you do irritates them and take it with the attitude with which you wish them to take your criticism. Suggest working on a solution so that it enables a better working relationship between you and so that you can both enjoy work without any kind of conflict.

The other person will then understand better why you withdraw from the relationship and can understand how he or she can help prevent the situation happening again. Remember: no one can read minds; communication is always the key to a successful conflict-free relationship.

Think before you speak: simple and to the point

You should think carefully about what you want to say and how you want it to come across. You need to keep your communication simple and concise, getting to the point whether you are communicating by e-mail, telephone, or face-to-face meetings. However, you must take care not to be perceived as aggressive when being concise, especially in e-mails. As a rule you should never enter into conflict situations when using e-mail.

The best way to resolve a conflict is face to face so that you can read the other person's body language as well as actively listen. You will notice when people are anxious, nervous or upset; their voice will become higher pitched and faster and they may often babble on, even when trying to communicate something simple.

Use a strong confident voice and reframe the problem

You should use a strong confident voice, and one of the most powerful ways to achieve that is to speak slowly.

Reframing the problem will trigger the mind to be creative and to think/do something different. Use the 'wonderful if' phrase: 'Wouldn't it be wonderful if...'. Use imagination and dreams to come up with many 'off the wall' ideas to help your creativity and then something sensible will come out of it. When dealing with conflict situations, there are certain words that would serve better than others in getting your point and feelings across (Table 4.1).

TABLE 4.1 Reframing the problem

Unhelpful phrases are:	Phrases to replace the unhelpful phrases are:
Yes, but...	Yes, and...
You should...	I need...
You are...	My perception is...
The blame lies with...	Let's find a solution to...
You are wrong...	My preference is... What I would like is... I disagree with you when you say...
You make me angry	I feel... when...

Ground rules for discussions

Be professional

Realize that the disagreement may be a good thing – a chance to clear the air, to solve a problem, to move things on and give you the opportunity to correct something that could have had dire consequences.

If you decide to discuss a problem with someone, arrange to hold the meeting in a neutral venue such as a conference room, not in either of your offices. You should prepare yourself thoroughly for the meeting – remember that 'If you fail to prepare you should prepare to fail.' Make brief notes of your key points. Understand the likely opposition and look for ways to defuse it. The goal is self-respect and a win–win situation. Give some thought to what an ideal decision or solution would accomplish. Instead of focusing on the situation as it is, you should be aiming to talk about the situation as you would like it to be. Focus on solutions and the future!

Clarify the matter right at the start – ask the question 'What exactly is the problem?' You may be able to solve it immediately if both of you come to understand exactly what the situation is. Half of all problems can be cleared up at this point. Take some time to be absolutely clear and really understand the items under discussion.

To do this, it is best to state what you need directly, whether it's more information, or help, or more time. Don't ask a question when you need to make a statement. For example, you should say 'I need another half an hour to complete that piece of work you want' rather than 'Could you please give me another half an hour to finish the piece of work?'

Remember to behave in an 'adult' way – remain objective, be confident, don't exaggerate, treat people with dignity and be tactful. It is important to respect the other person's feelings and give them a proper chance to talk without being interrupted. No matter how difficult you find it to keep your mouth shut – wait for your turn to speak. If you have to turn down a request, empathize with the person first as it softens the 'no': 'I understand your predicament but unfortunately the answer is still no.'

Be pleasant and agreeable as you talk with the other person. They may not be aware of the impact of their words or actions on you. In the worst case scenario they may know their impact on you and deny it, or explain it away by making excuses. It will help if you express appreciation, as telling others what you appreciate about them is a positive form of assertiveness.

Be assertive

'I' statements can help you be assertive without being critical. It is best to phrase your concerns in terms of what you need, not what's wrong with the other person. For example, saying 'I don't agree with what was said as I feel that...' is a more respectful way of saying 'You are wrong because...'. You should focus on your own experience of the situation rather than on attacking or accusing the other person. You can also explain to people the impact their actions have on you. These 'I' messages are a key part of assertive speaking that allows us to express negative feelings without attacking or blaming others, and helps to facilitate constructive dialogue and problem solving.

Similarly, using 'When' allows us to elicit indirect agreement. Instead of saying 'If', get used to saying 'When'. 'When we have decided that this is the best way of doing it, we will need to discuss how.'

When people are upset they often say things they don't mean and wouldn't normally have said – they become unreasonable. So for your part, try to keep your emotions under control and be forgiving. If the other person is emotional, asking questions helps them to fill in the blanks in their thinking until they become reasonable again.

Assertive people can disagree without being disagreeable – master the art of constructive disagreement and turn potential conflicts into problem-solving discussions. You may need to be flexible and willing to agree on a compromise and negotiate if appropriate. It is important to respond in the right way, control your emotions and avoid becoming defensive about your actions or territorial about your work. Know and believe you have rights; know and believe others have rights. These include, for example, being able to hold and express our own opinions and feelings, to be listened to, to be empathized with, to be taken seriously and to be treated with respect.

When we deal with conflict we should consider what our own needs are (how we feel; what we want from the outcome) and communicate these clearly and assertively to the other parties; at the same time we should consider their needs (how they feel; what they want from the outcome) and empathize with them.

Compromise

You should aim to find a compromise. Don't lay blame or make excuses, as that is unproductive. If it is appropriate, apologize and accept some or all of the responsibility. Compromising involves finding a mutually acceptable position where both parties give up some of the things they want and meet halfway. That is often the best outcome that can be expected in a conflict situation, especially where the goals (needs) of the parties are different.

Compromise can often be a win–win outcome where both parties work together in a mutually beneficial way by using the skills of listening (see Chapter 2 on listening skills), questioning, demonstrating empathy and building rapport.

Effective problem solving involves talking about the solutions instead of talking about the problems. The more you think and talk about solutions, the more positive and creative everyone will be and the better ideas you will come up with. A discussion of problems is inherently negative and demotivating, and tends to inhibit creativity. You can become a positive thinker simply by becoming a solution-oriented person rather than a problem-oriented one.

Strategies to help you deal with conflict and difficult characteristics of bosses

Don't take people's behaviour personally. It is likely that their difficult characteristics have become a habit and they will react the same way with most people. Realize and accept that if your boss gives you a tough time because he or she is stressed, it isn't personal. If the symptoms seem to occur only when the person is under stress, wait until another time to pursue the discussion.

Assistants are there to make their bosses' lives easier – so if bosses feel better for having had a rant (even if it isn't your fault) and they are then in a better frame of mind to win the business or perform better, then you are doing your job – **it isn't personal!**

Difficult people are not born difficult; they create and learn how to express these attitudes and behaviours, and because they are 'learnt' behaviours we can influence them to have better ones. Separating the behaviour from the person is the key to a successful working relationship. The bad behaviour may be temporary due to overwork or personal stress, or due to something as simple as lack of management skills. Understanding and empathizing with the underlying reasons means that your boss can save face and improve his or her behaviour appropriately.

When you deal with conflict, try to use both the logical left-hand side and the creative right-hand side of the brain. The more creative you are, the better the insights and the more ingenious the solution. Logical thought processes are enhanced by creativity, which comprises your imagination, intuition, 'brain connections' and good ideas that appear to just pop into your head. These thought processes occur when you are relaxed and doing things other than just concentrating on the problem in hand, like taking a shower or driving to work. At such times our brains tend to make connections and we get an 'Aha!' moment when we realize something, which is when the right-hand side of your brain is working together with your subconscious mind. Once you have identified the problem in your head, relax and let your subconscious mind work on it for you.

Your subconscious brain also works when you are asleep. You may have heard people say: 'Sleep on the problem and see how you feel about it in the morning – it will all become much clearer.' Try posing yourself a question before you go to sleep and remember to tell yourself: 'You don't need to think consciously about the problem because your subconscious will do it for you so you can get a good night's undisturbed sleep.' It's amazing how things are clearer in the morning and how often ideas pop into your head because your subconscious has been working on it throughout your sleep.

You can deal with difficult people by using 'emotional intelligence' (EI), which is a form of intelligence relating to the emotional side and entails being able to understand and having the skills to cope with your own emotions and feelings and those of others. You need to be self-aware, be able to motivate yourself, have emotional self-control and be able to empathize with others. Using EI you would be able to spot potential conflict, handle difficult people and tense situations with diplomacy and tact, bring disagreements into the open and defuse situations by encouraging open discussion that results in win–win solutions.

Dealing with difficult people takes practice, so don't get discouraged and do be tenacious with the strategies, tools and techniques that will help you deal with difficult characteristics of bosses and conflict management.

Beware of giving too much empathy

Empathizing and putting yourself in other people's shoes is to be recommended. However, you have to be careful that you do not neglect your own needs and feelings if you empathize too much, as this can lead to you becoming passive or timid.

Avoid apologizing too much

Some people tend to say 'I'm sorry' as a matter of habit and therefore their apologies can appear to be meaningless. If you are standing up for your rights and are being reasonable, there is no need to apologize.

Gaining clarity

We do not always come across to others in the way we mean to. Whatever has gone on in someone's past influences the way they think and the way they interpret what is being said to them. It is imperative that both parties understand exactly what each other means and to have clarity.

> *"To stop an argument say: 'Tell me what you think I just said... Now tell me what you think I meant.'"*
>
> (Richard Mullender, hostage negotiator trainer)

Change the way you react by using affirmations

You have to remember that you cannot fundamentally change people, though you can influence them to change their behaviours (and to do this you have to communicate constantly with them and feed back to them). You can, however, change yourself and the way you respond, and using affirmations is one way to do this. We use affirmations because our brains will respond to whatever we tell them. The affirmations go into our subconscious part of the brain where our deep-seated beliefs are kept.

Affirmations are statements that you repeat to yourself on a daily basis to increase your confidence and self-esteem, so that you believe them and your brain takes note of them. Thus they become your beliefs and your negative gremlins are changed or disposed of.

Some limiting beliefs have a lie within them – 'be **lie** fs' – so you shouldn't always believe your beliefs!

If you constantly tell yourself things like 'I can't ask for a rise because I'm not worthy' or 'My boss is going to be mad if I speak up' or 'It would be easier to just go along with them,' then you are only reinforcing your negative gremlins. To help tame the gremlins, use affirmations such as: 'From now on I will speak up for myself in an assertive way to get my point across calmly and succinctly.'

If people at work are annoying you, for whatever reason, and you have told them how you feel about it but they continue to act in the same way and are definitely being unreasonable, 'out of order' or disrespectful, you can change the way you react to them and whatever it is that upsets or annoys you by positive affirmations.

It's the way you respond to a situation that matters – don't just react! For example, some bosses might upset you by continually checking on you and looking over your shoulder to see if the work is done, even though they have not had any reason to doubt your efficiency from past experiences with you. First of all, you should tell them that their actions make you feel they don't trust you; that their interference is actually making you delay the delivery of the work; that you feel they lack confidence in your abilities. Assure them that you will tell them if the work cannot be done on time. If they continue to keep checking on you and chasing you for work, then you can change the way you respond to their actions and words. You should say to yourself:

> My boss's reactions are not going to affect me; I do not take it personally.
> I have confidence in my abilities and I will get the work done on time. It does
> not worry me that my boss feels a need to keep on monitoring me. It makes
> no difference to the way I work and eventually he or she will come to trust and
> appreciate me because I constantly deliver on time.

The way you respond to people at work can have a massive impact on your working life, happiness and effectiveness. We really do have an ability to change our responses and reactions to how other people affect us and our emotions.

If you prefer to make smaller affirmations that are easy to remember then you can simply keep saying to yourself: 'I am not taking anything said to me personally or to heart.' This is a powerful affirmation that you need to believe and act upon, as it can save a lot of heartache, unnecessary worry, wasted time and energy. Too often we do take things to heart and dwell upon what people have said to us, and later we think 'Why didn't I say this...?' 'Why didn't I say that...?' – we get more and more 'wound up' as we think about it, and our work and our professionalism can suffer.

E-mail rage

To deal with conflict, think through the reaction you want to give, take time to review the situation, try to put your emotions to the side and consider the outcome you desire. If, for example, you are about to send an angry e-mail reply to someone, then you should stop and think about picking up the phone and asking for a meeting with the person concerned. You should decide on a mutually convenient time, date and location. The meeting place should be in a neutral, private place, not in your office or in the other person's as this gives a psychological advantage. If a meeting is not possible then consider setting up a telephone conference call to discuss the situation. If these two methods fail then it is best to wait until you can have a face-to-face meeting. If for some reason you feel you have to send an e-mail, first keep it in draft format for a while, think about it and rewrite your draft until it is appropriate to send. In that way you can manage the conflict effectively so that the outcome is a 'win–win' situation for both parties.

Real-life case studies on how to deal with difficult bosses/conflict

Case study one

'My boss is very set in her ways and sometimes it's difficult for her to realize that I am here to do everything she can't or doesn't have time to do, and she will neglect to tell me about meetings and other things, which can make me look and feel unprepared.'

   Solution: Set up a shared calendar for such bosses, so that you can see all their appointments, and make sure that you meet with them at the end of each day to go through the next day's events, especially when something important is coming up or if they are about to travel. Also make sure you have sight of all correspondence.

Checking your boss's sent e-mails can be very informative.

Case study two

'Once there was a colleague who worked closely with my boss. I worked as a PA and also supported his team – including this particular colleague. We seemed to get along pretty well in the beginning but after a while my boss told me that the colleague had been criticizing me strongly. For example, he told him that I needed a course in PowerPoint as my presentations were not acceptable. He was the only one with this opinion and my boss also did not see any problem. My problem was that this colleague did not talk to me directly but went over my head. There were several incidents like that – at least several I know of. I talked to my boss about it and finally resigned from the job.'

Solution: Before resigning from the job it would be best to speak to the person concerned directly rather than through a third party, so that you could find out what exactly the problem was that he or she had with your work. You could use the problem-solving technique in Appendix 5. Also, we can all learn something new every day, even with the tools we use every day. I would always accept an offer of training in any subject (especially if the company is giving time off to do it and paying the fees and expenses). Even if the outcome was still your resignation, you would have had further training to add to your CV (for when you apply for new jobs) and you might understand why the colleague was behaving in that way.

Case study three

'A difficult characteristic of my boss was his timekeeping and his inability to start the working day on time! He was very good at starting the working day in the afternoon. How did I cope? By complementing his working style for the greater good of our clients, by being up to date and ready to go when he started to dictate and by planning my home life to fit around work.'

Solution: You should remember and realize that you have 'rights': the right to a work–life balance and the right to work within your contractual hours and be allowed to leave on time so that you have time for your family/ home/social life, just as your boss should be doing.

If you are assertive with your bosses on behalf of your own time it will also help them with their time management and may well save their work–life balance and personal relationships.

In this scenario you should assertively say to your boss:

> When you continually start dictating in the afternoon, it makes me feel that I have to stay late in order to fit in with your work style and consequently my family and social life are suffering. I will help you arrange the diary so that you are able to dictate in the morning in order to get your work done within the day. If this is going to be a problem for you I suggest we talk about it.

Bosses are not mind readers and may in fact think you prefer to work the way you have been doing. You have to let them know how you feel, come up with a solution and ask them what they think about it. Then you can work on the problem together to come to a workable solution.

Case study four

'I started as a PA in a new company. The head of administration services was a woman who'd worked for many years for the company and had a very close relationship with the CEO. Immediately, she saw me as real competition in the trust of our boss, and attacked with many tiny bullying methods during my trial period of six months. This was of course annoying, and one day when she had to deliver some documents to my home, I invited her to a joint leisure day at a later date. From her positive reaction, I discovered that she did not mean her attacks personally, and since then, even after I left the company, we have maintained a very close friendly relationship.'

Solution: Many people do indeed act differently in their business and their private lives, therefore remember to separate the behaviour from the person to help you understand. Most conflict situations tend to be misunderstood as personal attacks, although they are due to feelings of insecurity in people's business world.

Case study five

'One person has joined our department who was a PA in her previous job. This person constantly seems to think I need advice and constantly butts in with answers to questions directed at me. She also likes to keep everyone informed that she has already done it, seen it and knows it.'

Solution: Smile when people offer 'advice', thank them and then do it your way. When the advice offered is appropriate, thank them and change things – hopefully for the better.

Case study six

'One boss I used to work for had trouble in delegating.'

Solution: 'I introduced him to time management by using spreadsheets to let him see how much more time he would have if certain tasks were carried out by me: inbox management, diary management, minute-taking during management meetings and so on.'

Understanding your boss's work style and patterns can help overcome many of the communication and behaviour obstacles that you may encounter. At the same time, it is equally important to identify and understand your own work style as we have most difficulty understanding those whose preferences and styles of communication are different from our own.

Once you and your boss have discovered your personality types, highlighting strengths and weaknesses, you may both need to make some adjustments in communication/behaviour styles and address each other's strengths and weaknesses (although approaching the subject with your boss may require some caution!). You can then take the relevant steps to work towards a much more harmonious and enjoyable relationship.

Different types of management style

Whatever type of boss you work for there is one attribute you definitely need to cope with every single type of management style: a sense of humour!

The commander boss

The commander boss communicates in a direct, authoritative style, but is actually open to input. The commanders genuinely believe that they know all the right answers and expect everything to be done their way. They will mention something that they want you to do – however vaguely or passing in the corridor – and they will expect it done. They can never accept constructive criticism, no matter how you deliver it. They believe that their way of doing things is always correct, and nothing you or anyone else can say will ever change their minds.

How to deal with the commander boss: Acknowledge the value of your boss's ideas and approaches. Don't present your own opinions in a confrontational manner. Use questions to keep your boss from being defensive. Start your sentences with 'Do you think we might...?' or 'Could we consider...?' instead of 'We should...' or 'We have to...'. Never tell dictatorial managers that they 'can't' do something, because they can and will just to prove a point. Instead, try beginning your sentence with 'Yes, we can do that, but let me ask you something...' followed by whatever question or concern you may have. Amazingly enough, simply acknowledging their power usually keeps them calm. Make it happen. Once they have issued some vague directive, commanders don't want to hear about that issue again. In their mind, it has been dealt with – by giving it to you – and they have moved on to other matters. They will only return to it if something seems to be going wrong, and you don't want that kind of attention. Don't give them details; they are only interested in the big picture.

The negative boss

The negative boss is hardly ever positive and more likely to be pessimistic – the 'half-empty glass' type; the boss who thinks that 'it won't work', 'they won't accept that'.

How to deal with the negative boss: Use active listening skills until you are certain that negative bosses feel listened to and that you have heard them. Then decide whether they have legitimate reasons for their negativity and see where you can help them. Rephrase back to them what they have told you so that they know you have understood and they don't keep repeating themselves. Or if they do, simply finish off their sentence for them and say, 'Yes, I know, as I listened yesterday.' Know your limits and don't start trying to be their counsellor (or you'll start feeling negative yourself!). Short-term advice that points a person in a positive direction is fine, but for anything more than that, ask them to seek professional advice or visit Human Resources to solve their problem (or, if your company has one, an employee assistance programme).

Sometimes, they just want to talk. If you just listen – there's no need to offer advice – they will go away happy.

The boss who is new to the company

Newly arrived bosses don't know much about their new environment but you should accept the fact that they will have new ideas to bring in. They do have a past and they may well have been at the top of their game – respect that.

How to deal with the new boss to the company: Read Chapter 1 on how to build a relationship with new bosses. They need your help and support to settle in and learn the processes and traditions. As they are new to the environment they will be open to information, ideas and suggestions. Make sure that they don't make any decisions without informed knowledge, information and an understanding of the relevant policies and procedures. Do not be condescending and be sure to show respect for the knowledge or experience that they have from their past experiences. Create a list of questions you want to ask them and ask for a list of things that irritate them and things that they would like you to do, then set up a time to meet to discuss.

If possible, contact your boss's former assistant and find out all you can, such as how they like their e-mails and Outlook Calendar organized and even preferences for travel and accommodation – anything that was important to them.

The bully boss

The bully occasionally gets upset and yells, but then calms down, talks rationally and may even apologize. Bullying can take many forms, such as enjoying verbally abusing others, teasing, sarcasm and humiliation. Any prolonged behaviour that makes it unbearable for you to work can be considered bullying.

How to deal with the bully boss: With mild bullies, avoid the natural fight-or-flight reaction and remain in a calm, rational mode. People feel stupid being angry by themselves, so the boss will usually calm down and may be willing to engage in a discussion. Don't take any mild abuse personally. If you're forced to deal with a boss who yells and is insulting, remember not to take it personally, as this is just a boss with bad manners. You should always be assertive and remember that you have rights. Bullies are adept at knowing and exploiting your weak points. Confuse them by behaving in an assertive, strong manner, even if you don't feel that way inside. And no matter how hard they push, don't show them you're upset. It's no fun bullying someone who doesn't react, and so the bad behaviour often stops.

For bullies in the true sense of the word, go to their boss or HR and have a word to see what your best options are – possibly a transfer to another department. Keep your self-confidence and self-belief and show them that you are confident while respectfully acknowledging their authority.

If the conflict is still not resolved or if it is of a serious nature such as sexual harassment, then you should check your company policy on grievance procedures and take the matter through the proper channels according to your company grievance procedures policy.

It is also advisable to take notes, noting time, date and what was said by whom to whom, in case these should be needed in a grievance procedure. If you can get the other person involved to sign these notes as a true account of the meeting, then that is better. However, just the fact that they know you are making such notes may help them to want to find a mutual workable compromise.

"No one can make you feel inferior without your consent!"
(Eleanor Roosevelt)

The controller boss

Controller bosses are people who are highly anxious about making mistakes. They are reluctant to give up control and therefore feel a need to be involved in every detail of your work. They will check up on you and keep asking you if something has been done, instead of trusting you to get it done when asked for. Sometimes they are only like this when you first start working together and they have not yet begun to trust you. There is also the possibility that the boss is not happy with your performance and feels the need to closely manage you. Taking control and watching, checking every step you make, gives controller bosses a reassuring feeling that the correct steps are being taken and that the task will be completed correctly and on time. They rarely delegate a project to you. The controller boss can irritate you and may eventually make you lose the ability to think or function for yourself.

How to deal with the controller boss: You need to make such bosses comfortable with your work style and to gain their trust by always delivering on time. Be proactive and provide reassurance by reporting back to them the steps you've taken and where you are up to. Reassure them that the task is being done correctly and you will deliver on time. Inform them, especially on issues that you know are important to them, without being asked. Try to anticipate their needs and what they want to know, and have regular update meetings and discuss possible concerns about projects. Once you have begun to gain their trust, discuss the possibility of their empowering you with a project where you can make decisions independently, reassuring them that you will always keep them informed.

Regardless of which type of management style or combination of styles bosses have, one way to influence their behaviour is to talk to them and make them aware of their behaviour and how it affects you and how it makes you feel. More importantly, you have to communicate how you would prefer them to behave.

When you catch yourself feeling defensive, don't react so quickly but learn to respond, as it is difficult to change people; but you can influence the way they behave by the way you respond.

Remember to be assertive in appropriate situations, say affirmations to keep your self-confidence and use the problem-solving technique in Appendix 5 to help you to be systematically creative. Look realistically at risks and benefits in order to solve any problem.

The effort you make to improve your ability to get along with others will be rewarded as you find more projects and career opportunities open up for you.

Time, organizing and stress management

05

Time/task management

Stress is what we feel when we cannot cope with pressure. It can cause damage to your health and your relationships both at work and at home. Having controlled pressure, in contrast, helps to raise adrenalin levels, gets your brain working and gives you energy.

> Plan your time and organize your tasks so that you can get the right things done at the right time and in the right way, resulting in feeling in control and stress free.

Assistants have to work on many different tasks every day: opening the mail, sorting and replying to e-mails, organizing travel, organizing events, claiming your boss's expenses, answering the phone, taking/typing minutes, finding the files and folders your boss needs, taking dictation, creating documents/ presentations, preparing agendas, collating documentation and maps for meetings, booking couriers, greeting clients, working on special projects, diary management and much more. The way to cope with our multitasking skilled jobs is with:

- time or task management skills;
- organizational skills;

- effective use of e-mail management;
- stress management;
- teamwork;
- delegation.

You have not only got to manage your own time but also that of your boss(es). Making the most effective use of your time and theirs is imperative to a successful working relationship and a satisfying job well done.

Prioritizing the workload

Prioritizing should take into account your goals and objectives. Carmen Pérez Pies, EUMA, Germany, advises: 'Constant communication and updates with your boss are imperative so that you can align your priorities to match theirs.'

Methods to help prioritize work

Handwritten to-do lists

Always write everything down; keep your to-do list/Outlook task list etc in front of you and add to it as necessary. Writing everything down stops you from worrying. Tick off items as you complete them (ticking them off makes you feel good as things get done). If things can wait until the next day then put them in the next day's to-do list.

If you are the type of person who might wake up in the middle of the night remembering things you should have done or you have to do, then keep a pad and pen by your bed, write it down and get it off your mind. This will enable your mind to rest and then you can have a good night's sleep, which is important to enable you to function 100 per cent the next day.

Sometimes it is prudent to check your list and ask questions in case you can delete some of them. Use the 'Four Ds' to remove an item from your to-do list:

Deal with it (which could include filing it away).

Delete it/Dump it (binning any hard-copy documentation).

Delegate it – write down to whom, when given out and when expected back.

Defer it (use your reminder systems).

To-do lists could include the time/date/estimation of time it will take to do the task, the results you wish to achieve and actions required, such as people you need to speak with or meetings you need to attend. You can use highlighter pens and colour code items in order of priority.

Computerized calendar/tasks

Programs such as Outlook use the alarm warning system. You can colour these in to help you prioritize.

> In order to remember to action the thoughts that pop into your head during the day or night, as soon as you think of it, write it down or type it.

Follow-up systems

There are various follow-up/reminder systems, such as concertina-type files with daily compartments for maps, documents, travel tickets and so on.

You can use a combination of the computerized 'calendar' and 'tasks' with alarms to appear at certain times on certain days. Some could remind you to check hard-copy 'reminder follow-up' systems to retrieve the documents needed that day. Remember to put reminders on your boss's desk the night before, in case you are not in work early the next morning or if you fall ill. You should inform your boss of how the filing and reminder systems are organized and where they are in case you are not available when they need something.

Desk trays

You can label the trays in whatever way suits you best: for example, 'important/urgent', 'today' and 'pending'.

> To prevent procrastination and to be productive, the key question you should ask yourself repeatedly throughout the day is: Is this the best use of my time, right now?

Approaches to prioritizing

Lisa Rodgers, a past *Times* Crème/Hays PA of the Year winner, says:

> A most challenging aspect of my job is juggling a large workload. I couldn't survive without my to-do list and diary. I plan my day over a cup of coffee in the morning and review it at the end of the day, carrying over uncompleted tasks. It's the only way to know where I'm at with all my different projects.

When you are prioritizing your boss's diary you have to consider making time for personal activities and for getting away from work on time to enable both your boss and yourself to have a work–life balance. You may need to diarize time for bosses to be at their children's school play/school assembly, parents' evening, evening classes, sports events and so on.

> *"I will sometimes put all my papers into one pile, re-sift and re-sort, get a drink, then re-prioritize accordingly. I usually find I'm not as bombarded as I previously felt I was."*
>
> (Cheryl Sykes)

Stephen R Covey made the four-quadrant approach of Roger and Rebecca Merrill famous. In a matrix, every goal or activity can be placed in one of four quadrants:

1 Important and urgent.

2 Important but not urgent.

3 Not important but urgent.

4 Not important and not urgent.

While the first quadrant (Important and urgent) needs to be tackled first, the best time management tool is doing what's important *before* it becomes urgent, which can be achieved by using the second quadrant.

I have adapted this idea as shown in Figure 5.1 and Figure 5.2 – a task prioritization matrix guide that helps to prioritize your work into an order in which tasks should be completed each day. You will find this plus the blank matrix form online for you to download and use as your daily to-do list. For details please see the front of the book.

The task prioritization matrix

Figure 5.1 shows a matrix that can be used for prioritizing tasks each day. Once you have downloaded the blank matrix, you can complete it on the computer so that it is easy to carry forward tasks that you have not been able to do today. At the end of the day you could delete all the tasks that

FIGURE 5.1 Task prioritization matrix

'Do the right things at the right time in the right way'
Deal with it, Delegate it, Delay it or Dump it

	Urgent	Less urgent	
Important tasks	**1st priority – Do now** AM PM	**2nd priority – Plan today** AM PM	**Important tasks**
Less important tasks	**3rd priority – Do today** AM PM	**4th priority – Don't forget to do it or dump it!** Include deadline date too	**Less important tasks**
	Urgent	Less urgent	

have been completed (what a lovely feeling) and move the remaining tasks for the next day into their appropriate area, as things may become important and urgent. In the morning you could add more tasks, creating a new task prioritization matrix for that day:

1 Important/urgent tasks. These are your first priority – 'Do now'.
   Highly important and urgent tasks must be done first. This category

FIGURE 5.2 Task prioritizing matrix guide

'Do the right things at the right time in the right way'

	Urgent	Less urgent	
Important tasks	**1 Do now – top priority** Highly important and urgent tasks must be done first and this would include unforeseen emergencies and deadlines. **1st golden rule of time management – ask yourself:** **'Is this the best use of my time right now?'**	**2 Plan today – second priority** High importance value but less urgent – these tasks need to be planned, thought through, researched and support information collected to enable them to be conducted effectively and efficiently. Twenty per cent of these tasks done each day without interruption can generate 80 per cent of the key results. The more time spent on this category means the less likelihood of 'Urgent/ Important task crisis' arising. Tasks include proactivity, preparation, research, prevention and maintenance, thereby facilitating productivity, excellent relationships and high quality.	**Important tasks**
Less important tasks	**3 Do today – third priority** Less important but urgent tasks need to be managed to avoid them becoming more important tasks. Urgent does not always mean NOW but could mean today at some point! Ask questions to help prioritize and position the task in the working day, eg 'When is the latest I can get it to you?' so that you can buy time for quadrants 1 and 2. Put them in today's 'to-do' list to remind you to do them at the appropriate time.	**4 Don't forget to do** Less important and not urgent. These tasks can be done by a stated deadline or when a suitable 'hole in the day' arises. **2nd golden rule of time management:** **Never do lower-value tasks at high-energy-level time**	**Less important tasks**
	Urgent	Less urgent	

would include unforeseen emergencies and deadlines. When planning your day you should leave some 'cushion' time for unforeseen but possible emergencies and interruptions.

2   Important but less urgent tasks. This category is your second priority – 'Plan for today'. These tasks need to be planned, thought through, researched, and support information collected to enable them to be performed effectively and efficiently. Just 20% of these tasks done each day without interruption can generate 80% of the key results.

The more time spent on this category, the less likelihood there is of 'Urgent/important' task crises arising. Tasks include proactivity, preparation, research, prevention and maintenance, which will facilitate productivity, excellent relationships and high quality.

Once you put these time management solutions in place and begin working efficiently, you will have fewer or no urgent things to do, as you will have done them before they become urgent. They only become urgent because of procrastination and leaving them until the last minute.

3 Less important and urgent tasks. This is your third priority – 'Do today'. These tasks need to be managed to avoid them becoming more important. Urgent does not always mean now but could mean today at some point. Ask questions to help prioritize and position the task in the working day – for example, 'When is the latest I can get it to you?' – so that you can buy time for quadrants 1 and 2. Put them in today's to-do list to remind you to do them at the appropriate time.

4 Less urgent/less important. Don't forget to do these tasks – they can be carried over to the next day or to their deadline date. These tasks can be done by a stated deadline or when a suitable 'hole in the day' arises. Sometimes these tasks may not need to be done at all and can be deleted.

Once you have decided which items are important (or not) and urgent (or not), then you need to prioritize the order in which those tasks have to be done within each quadrant.

The nature of the job is that you will be multitasking all the time. However, to deal with important urgent tasks and to be most effective, you need to focus your concentration on one thing at a time and get it completed, or to the stage that you need it to be, before tackling another pressing task. You will inevitably be disturbed by requests from the boss or by telephone calls but you have to get back immediately to the important and urgent task in hand and complete it. You have to be tenacious when tackling such jobs. You should accept interruptions as part of the job and not let them irritate you.

"*Efficiency is doing things right; effectiveness is doing the right things.*"
(Peter Drucker)

To do the right things, you need to align your goals with those of your boss and your organization. You then have to put the right things on your to-do list in the right order and allocate the right amount of time to each task. However, you should always allow extra time for preparing your task, for interruptions and for other unforeseen and more important/urgent tasks taking priority. We have approximately 7.5 hours in our working day and if you feel that you don't have time to do some tasks, it simply means that you have chosen to do something else. Therefore it is important that you make sure you are choosing the right option.

As a golden rule of time management, always use your high-energy time for your most difficult and arduous tasks, as then you will find them easier to deal with.

To help you to realize the order the tasks should be completed in and to determine which are important and urgent, you should think about the following three words: 'because', 'by' and 'why':

- This task is important and urgent *because*... For example: The client is coming in to collect the documentation, which I must have typed up and sitting on the reception desk ready for collection.

- It needs to be done *by*... For example: The client is coming in at 12 noon.

- The reason *why* the client needs it is... For example: They need it for the court hearing this afternoon.

Once you understand the 'because, by and why' of the task, it will be easier to focus on getting it completed and meeting the deadline.

The wonderful thing about setting priorities and concentrating single-mindedly is that you will begin to feel a tremendous sense of achievement and well-being. As you work progressively towards the accomplishment of all of your most important urgent tasks, you will feel a flow of energy and enthusiasm. As you finish something that is significant for yourself, your boss or your organization, your self-esteem improves and you feel that you are making a difference, which encourages you to carry on until you have completed all your tasks.

Look for time-wasting activities and situations that you could manage differently so as to improve your time management. Also look for duplication of effort to cut your wasted time by half, and see if there are any tasks that you could delegate.

We all need to make the most of the precious hours we have available to us both within and outside work. We often think to ourselves 'I've been really busy today but I have not achieved everything I wanted to.' The next section will help you to analyse your 'time thieves' and to concentrate on what is important so that you can achieve what you need to get done in a given day.

'Time thieves'

You need to identify the time thieves and take control of them, delegate them or eliminate them. One way to identify them is to keep a time log of how you actually use your time. This would be more detailed than your to-do list as it would include things like chatting to the assistant in the next department for 20 minutes or fixing the photocopier that is always breaking down. Analyse your time log, reflect on what you have discovered and think about what changes you can make to improve your time management.

Time thieves include:

inability to say 'No';	fire-fighting;
your boss;	lack of filing;
your colleagues;	lack of planning;
lack of motivation;	miscommunication and stress;
misunderstanding;	procrastination;
work you could have delegated;	indecisiveness;
lack of knowledge;	the telephone;
inadequate tools;	meetings;
inadequate information;	lack of prioritization;
tiredness and lack of sleep;	untidy desk;
concentration;	

> visitors (invited and uninvited – make sure you agree on a set length of time for the meeting and stick to that time).

Another group of thieves are the negative gremlins. Negative feelings and negative self-talk drain our energy and prevent us from being more productive. Work on your internal dialogue to be more positive and do not dwell on anything that has gone wrong in the past. See more on this in Chapter 3.

The following suggestions will help you manage time thieves:

- Focus on the future, not the past. After all, which one can you change?

- Be creative: increase/stretch the task's challenge or goal to get you motivated so that you rise to the challenge and exceed expectations.

- Set the tone for the whole day by ensuring that you are productive in the first two hours (this is probably when your energy is highest).

- Be proactive instead of reactive.

- Have your positive coach tell yourself 'I will get this done on time' and get rid of the negative gremlins that are chipping away at you, making you procrastinate and telling you that you haven't got enough time. (See more on the positive coach and negative gremlins in Chapter 3.)

- Delegate – including the jobs you like doing and not just the jobs you dislike doing. Think 'out of the box' about who you can delegate to.

- Have realistic expectations of what you can achieve, then achieve them.

- Ensure that meetings organized for your boss or for yourself are short, well planned and focused, and have clear outcomes.

- Establish a routine for dealing with regular jobs.

- Have a clear vision and goals (see more on goals in Chapter 3).

- Have a well-defined day, with what you have to do clearly established.

- Avoid the 'I'll just put this here for now' habit.

- Think creatively about how you can get rid of time thieves to meet deadlines.

For example: Avoid the 'I'll just put this here for now' habit. If you have an open office and you need to stop people from either disturbing you or your boss, you should have a hook on the wall near your or your boss's desk. When you can be interrupted you can hang a green card up, when you are busy and can be disturbed for only urgent matters you can hang an orange card on the wall, and when you should not be disturbed at all you can hang a red card on the wall.

Your desk

Keep your desk tidy and be able to find files, folders and information quickly and easily (a tidy desk gives you a tidy mind). Your desk should also be ergonomically tested so that it is laid out in the best way to help with your time management. For example, if you are right-handed your phone should be on your left-hand side and a pad and pen should be on your right. This enables you to be able to pick the handset up easily and quickly with your left hand, leaving your right hand free to find your pen and pad to write messages without twisting your body. (See more on ergonomics in Chapter 8.)

Interruptions

Learn to manage interruptions by being assertive, using body language and so on. For example, if people come to your desk to chat when you are busy, you have to tell them that you'd love to come and see them later but just now you have to meet a deadline and need to get on with your work – and check that they are not busy when you want to see them. Use body language to show them you're not available to chat by standing up and looking as if you're going somewhere. If you have your own office, walk them to the door.

Set limits on tasks and deal with them cleanly

Make sure you have limits to your work. For instance, promise yourself that you will only look at e-mails in half-hour chunks every three hours, or promise yourself you will work on Project X for two hours in the afternoon.

Only pick up a piece of paper once and deal with it by working on it, binning it, delegating it or filing it – do not keep picking it up and putting it on another part of your desk or back on its pile again to deal with later.

Avoid procrastination

Most people procrastinate to some degree and it stops you achieving your goals for the day. The key to overcoming procrastination is to:

- recognize when you start procrastinating;
- understand why it happens (even to the best of us);
- take active steps to better time management.

Procrastination happens when you:

- feel overwhelmed by a task, not knowing where to begin;
- are disorganized;
- put off things in favour of doing something you enjoy doing or that is within your comfort zone – something you know you will be able to complete easily;
- don't understand the difference between urgent tasks and important tasks, and do the urgent tasks that are not important;
- think you have not got the skills, knowledge or resources required to complete the task;
- think you have more time than you actually do, and have no concept of how time flies;
- are waiting to feel in the mood to tackle it, so you keep putting it off as you never do feel like doing it;

- negative gremlins are putting obstacles in your way and telling you that you won't be able to do it, it's too difficult, it's time consuming so you may as well get other things out of the way first – any excuse not to do it because of lack of self-belief.

How to overcome procrastination

 Don't put off until tomorrow what you can do today.

- Be honest with yourself and acknowledge when you procrastinate (everyone procrastinates at some time). Then you will more easily recognize when you are doing it.
- Work from your planned to-do list (or your personalized and completed 'task prioritization matrix') and don't just do low-priority tasks.
- Ask yourself: 'What is the consequence of not doing the task?' What could happen at your next appraisal because you haven't done it?
- Motivate yourself to do the task. For example, promise yourself a reward when it's completed: maybe some chocolate or a new outfit – any excuse to shop!
- Realize what the benefit of completing the task is to you – it may be that you have learnt how to do something new.
- If you have a coach or a mentor, ask for their help in setting deadlines and holding you accountable. Once other people know about a target and you have said out loud that you will do it and by when, you set up a contract with yourself and feel psychologically obliged to get it done.
- Break the project into micro tasks that are more manageable; do some of the tasks that give you immediate results to motivate you to do more. For example, make a deal with yourself and do the task you have been putting off in chunks of, say, 15 minutes.

Organizational skills

Organizational skills are paramount for successful time management. Lisa Rodgers, a past *Times* Crème/Hays PA of the Year believes that:

> A successful assistant should be seen as the most organized person in the company. You need to know where to find a file/document at the drop of a hat – a difficult task for someone who isn't organized and has a ton of paperwork on and around their desk. Keeping a to-do list and planning your own diary/time will make life a lot easier. If you can organize yourself, you can organize anybody. Time management and prioritization skills need to be honed in order to manage somebody else's workload as well as your own. You must instinctively know where everything is.

Patience is a virtue, especially for an assistant – adapt in some ways to your boss's work style and keep trying until you reach an agreed compromise! However, in most circumstances it is best to have organization in your work station, desk and cupboards – to be neat, tidy, in order and ergonomically correct.

Top tips for managing deadlines

- Insist that there will be no false deadlines – remind your boss that if a deadline is set you want to see the product being dealt with, and if necessary put time in the diary to deal with it.

- Only agree deadlines for yourself, never for your colleagues without checking with them first.

- Insist on bosses being specific when giving deadline dates and times. Do not allow them to use 'as soon as possible' (ASAP) or 'urgent' as this is too imprecise for you to be able to prioritize effectively or efficiently.

- Understand the reason for the deadline and the consequences of missing it. That will ensure that you prioritize effectively and give the task the attention it deserves in the most appropriate way.

- When you ask other people to do something, always give a time and date when you need it, as this gives them an incentive/goal to work towards.

- Do not accept deadlines like 'First thing Monday' when told on Friday at 5 pm. Everyone knows that you won't deal with whatever it is overnight or at the weekend (or at least you shouldn't!). Accept deadlines that are more meaningful, for example Monday 3 pm or Tuesday 10 am.

- Write the deadline down on your task prioritization form, to-do list or task list on the computer so that it is kept in mind.

- Remember to give deadlines to your boss. For instance, when you have to leave on time and you know that your boss has a piece of work that has to be completed that day, remind him or her that you will be leaving on time and the piece of work should be with you by, say, 3.30 pm at the latest so that it can be completed that day.

- Don't leave it to the last minute to chase a really important deadline.

Top 10 ways to save time dealing with e-mail

Here are 10 ways to impress your boss with your e-mail management skills (tips from Dr Monica Seeley):

- Don't be a slave to the new e-mail notification(s) such as the ping, the box that flashes across the screen telling you that you have new e-mails. Switch them off so that you are not distracted, then check for new e-mails when you are ready.

- Avoid dipping in and out whenever possible. Instead set aside specific times for dealing with e-mail.

- Handle each e-mail once and follow the Four Ds principle – deal with it, delete it, delegate it or defer action.

- Establish a reliable system for tracking e-mails that still need action, such as flags or creating a task.

- Use colour codes to identify e-mails from important people.

- Prioritize and use rules to sort less important e-mails as they arrive (eg 'out of' messages and newsletters).

- Keep within 75% of your mailbox limit. Do your e-mail housekeeping regularly and at least once a week: delete old e-mails, clear out the sent items and save important attachments to a file outside the e-mail system (eg file on the network).

- Attach first, then write the e-mail. I have received (and even sent) many e-mails without the relevant attachment. Attaching first then writing the e-mail avoids this embarrassing situation and saves everyone's time.

- Write a clear, precise subject line that accurately reflects the content, and include the date by which you need a response (eg Agenda for 23 March Board Meeting – action by 2 March).
- Use shortcut keys – examples are below:
  - Send and receive e-mail: CTRL+M.
  - New message: CTRL+N.
  - Delete an e-mail message: DEL or CTRL+D.
  - Reply to the message author: CTRL+R.
  - Reply to all: CTRL+SHIFT+R.
  - Forward a message: CTRL+F.
  - Find a message: CTRL+SHIFT+F.
  - Print the selected message: CTRL+P.

There are many more e-mail time management ideas and if you know them you should share them. If you don't know them you should research them and then share them!

> "One of my bosses has a tendency to not do their e-mails and will wander off to talk to someone or do anything other than reply to them. I deal with this by making sure I put 'e-mail time' in the diary or I will reduce the amount of e-mails by filing and printing off e-mails/documents that just need to be read for info and ones that need replies. Then I will sit with my boss and go through them. If some still aren't dealt with I will hound the boss until they are!"

Stress management

This section deals with emotional stress; please see Chapter 8 on ergonomics for stress-related issues to do with muscular, visual and environmental demands.

> "I have been through some really terrible stressful things in my life... some of which actually happened."
>
> (Mark Twain)

There is a difference between being prepared/organized and being stressed about something that might go wrong, that might happen, that might... I think the motto here is: 'Don't worry about things until they actually go wrong, but do think ahead and make contingency plans to make sure everything happens the way you want it to, even if it does end up being "plan B"!'

As long as you feel in control and are happy to be coping, there is no problem. Respect other people's optimum level of pressure, whether it is lower or higher than your own, and work out what your personal level of achievement is. Stretch yourself and see how far you can go – you may be pleasantly surprised!

Pressure only becomes stress when we lose control and then we start to panic. Once you lose control, pressure becomes stress and affects your ability to work effectively.

When the pressure is greater than your ability to cope, it's time to assess your lifestyle and work practices and see what you can do to minimize stress. The source may be work related or personal, or a blend of both, but the key is realizing that you are stressed and taking action to take the pressure off; if necessary, talk to someone about it.

> "I cope with the stress primarily by accepting that there is always some stress attached to a job, as there is to life in general, but I try to manage my time the best I can by being organized and proactive and making sure that my work–life balance is as good as I can make it. I never take work home with me; that is my first rule and always has been in all my jobs, and to be able to do that I make sure that I give 120 per cent during the day.'"

(Brigitte Thethy)

We all have different thresholds for stress. Some thrive on challenges and having lots of projects to do at once; the pressure makes adrenalin rise and they feel super-efficient and can get things done. Others couldn't cope with the same level of pressure.

When we are working at the right level of pressure, we can accomplish much more in a given time. It makes us feel satisfied that we are coping under pressure and getting lots done efficiently, which in turn enables us to do even more. This is why we should work at achieving 'stretched' goals, those that are a little harder than we think we could do comfortably. By stretching ourselves to go the extra mile we gain extra internal resources and move into a higher level of achievement, which gives us a thrill of excitement as we achieve more, learn more and can even become more creative.

Stress management requires that you take complete control over the activities of your daily life.

Examples of stress causers are:

- insufficient training and opportunities to learn new skills;
- poor work–life balance;

- lack of control over work;
- too much work or responsibilities;
- self-inflicted pressure – the stress of not knowing when to stop;
- organizational restructuring, changes in job;
- lack of ability to accept change;
- lack of teamwork;
- lack of respect;
- the words we use: for example, use 'could' instead of 'should', as using 'could' is a much more empowering word than 'should', which could make you feel guilty and therefore stressed.

"Stress at work occurs when you have no control over the circumstances in which you are working, usually deadlines. Take a few minutes to plan and prioritize, then tackle the most important thing first. Do the things that you personally have to do, then delegate the rest."
(Christine Davies, co-founder of EUMA)

Time management and lowering stress levels

The Pareto principle

The Pareto principle is sometimes referred to as the 'vital few' or 'the trivial many', and is more commonly known as the '80/20 rule'. It states that in anything you do, a few activities (20 per cent) are vital and many (80 per cent) are trivial.

It is useful to keep that in mind when you are faced with a number of alternatives. Ask yourself which items are the significant ones, as 20 per cent of the tasks in front of you are the vital, urgent and important tasks that have to be done first and 80 per cent can wait.

Remember to concentrate on results rather than on being busy. When you are prioritizing within the important/urgent box, think which 20 per cent of the things you have to do will produce 80 per cent of the results and do those first as they will make you feel that you have accomplished a job well done.

Tips for time management

- Learn to be appropriately assertive.
- Create or use company templates rather than making up documents every time.

- Don't take on more than you are able to do realistically.

- Use technology and social media to save time; for example, you can use 'Dropbox' for storing and sharing files as you can access them from anywhere.

- Take time to review your goals and objectives to help you keep on track.

- Take action for the right reason – make sure it's linked to your job or your objectives. You need to understand exactly what is expected of you.

- Review systems and procedures to make sure they are time effective. Make them simple, self-explanatory and flexible, and make sure everyone knows how they work and how to use them.

- Commit to setting time aside during the day to handle paperwork.

- Ensure that your work is achievable within realistic timeframes and deadlines and that you have adequate resources to do the job. Speak to your boss and possibly colleagues to see if you can delegate work or eliminate non-essential tasks.

- Have lists of things you are 'waiting for' from others and keep control of them by communicating your timelines clearly and chasing them appropriately.

- Batch together tasks of similar work, which may enable you to get through them faster.

- Define days or hours as admin, action, filing etc and let people know so that you can get on with the task undisturbed.

- Keep things in perspective. Ask yourself this question in order to lower your stress levels:

  - On a scale of 1–10 – and '10' is death! – just exactly how bad is the situation you are in right now? This should make you realize that whatever is causing you high levels of stress is, in fact, in the big scheme of things, not nearly as bad as you thought.

- Keep a reminder file for documents (if appropriate) and make it a habit to check your reminder file every morning as soon as you arrive so that you have all your papers together on the day they are needed. If you finish that day's documents, you can move on to the next day if appropriate.

"The things that matter most must never be at the mercy of the things that matter least."

(Goethe)

- Accept change, embrace it and go with it. It usually does work out for the better, especially when you are actively influencing any change that is happening.
- Use humour to reduce stress levels – have an attitude of fun.

Laughter

'Laughter is the best medicine and antidote to stress!' After a good laugh your blood pressure drops and your heart rate slows down. You will breathe more deeply and you will feel calmer.

Using time well

Do the things you least want to do early in the day. Use the following memory jogger to help you: 'BANJOE' – 'Bang A Nasty Job Off Early'. This will prevent you from procrastinating, reduce the pressure and stress from thinking about the 'nasty' job and letting it worry you while trying to do other tasks, and it will get it out of the way to give you a better day.

Use your most productive time effectively: do the most difficult jobs or the ones that need the most problem-solving skills or concentration when you work at your best. For me this is around 9.30 am to 12 noon, and I usually get another burst around 3.00 to 4.30 pm – it's all to do with biorhythms.

Similarly, identify the times when you are less productive, such as straight after lunch when your body is working hard to digest the food you have just eaten. Use these times to do the more mundane tasks such as managing your inbox, deleting your e-mails or catching up on some filing.

Take regular exercise, and take your lunch hour as the break will help you be more proactive in the afternoon. Include your personal time in your diary, and make sure you take your half-hour for a break as you will be more energized in the afternoon if you do so. Also note your finishing time and complete your work so that you can leave on time for your own appointment – home. Remember, the work–life balance is important.

Use your quiet time effectively – review your plans for accomplishing your goals and change your plans if necessary. Review your to-do list and priorities, check your reminder file.

Using your network

Know your limitations. Stay in control, even if you do want to please people, and always ask for help if necessary. Get help when you need it and work as a team. Delegate if you can, and when other people need help offer them assistance; in that way reciprocation will continue.

Sometimes it is appropriate for you to divert your phone so that you are not interrupted, but always be prepared to cover phones for others when they need your help.

Achievement and reward

Learn to set realistic expectations and appreciate your own achievements. Try to see the great things that you've accomplished, not the few things that may have been left undone.

It's always good to reward yourself when you have succeeded in completing certain projects or tasks. Give yourself a pat on the back if you have managed to prioritize and complete all the tasks you set out to do that day, or if you have reached one of your goals. This could mean buying yourself new clothes or just promising yourself a pampering bath when you get home, or a cosy night in – whatever it is that takes your fancy.

Advice on stress from around the world

Cheryl Sykes:

> Having so many loose details that need to be tied together and waiting for people to give you answers are a real challenge. I try to tie off as many loose ends as I can, while chasing for the missing answers early to avoid last-minute panic. Then I can cope with just one or two missing details at deadline.

Francoise Cumming:

> Have a life outside the office. You should never think that your life is the office.

Aman Malhotra:

> Cooperate with your staff (teamwork). If you have one or more co-workers who are willing to assist you in times of stress it will definitely reduce your stress level. And remember that you also have to help them when they are in need.

Hanne Vinther, Denmark:

> Prioritize your tasks and obtain extensions of deadlines if needed. (If you do not ask for an extension, you won't get it.)

Liz O'Farrell:

I keep each 'active' task or job in its own folder (electronically and physically); that way I know I can instantly lay my hands on all the details related to that job and work on them in order of priority, which changes constantly.

Kristy Stewart:

Take regular time out to prioritize your workload and you may find that you are stressed about nothing!

Carmen Perez Pies:

Take a break if possible. Remove yourself from the situation. Take a step back, gain perspective, get some fresh air, go for a coffee, go to the gym, have a cry in private if necessary, or just stomp around outside the building for a few minutes. As a golfer I find that a weekly session at the driving range in my lunch break works wonders – especially if I name each ball before I hit it.

Gillian Richmond, past European chairman for EUMA:

When stress levels hit a high, I find a 15-minute walk outside in the fresh air can work wonders. When you return, you feel refreshed and ready to pick up the challenge again, and the time away from your desk can be valuable in assembling your thoughts and priorities.

Carole Rigney:

Learn how to say 'No' and mean it! If someone asks you to do something for them and you already have a million things to do, you can either tell them that you could do it but not until a week on Friday (for example) or instead you can say, 'I can't do it at the moment but it might be quicker and easier if you do it' – then tell them what they need to know or do to complete the work themselves. This works particularly well if it's just a case of knowing who they need to ring to get something done.

Sarah Crown:

Start one job and finish it before going on to the next. It is very easy to suddenly realize you are juggling about five different tasks at the same time and then you get in a muddle (we have all done it and some of us still do). Where you need to leave a task to start another one, simply clip the paperwork together with a clear note of what still needs to be done with it so it is easy to pick up and carry on with it later.

Don't be afraid to ask for help. You may not get any, but if you don't ask you don't get. Maybe your colleague is not very busy and can help you out. He or she may be happy to do so, knowing you'll return the favour sometime.

Lesley Watts, past UK chairman for EUMA:

To cope with stress at work I try not to pick up on the negative vibes. I concentrate on my own role and then I can feel confident that I am doing a good job despite what might be going on around me.

Sarah Hewson:

> Keep work in perspective. Aim to do the best job you can when you are in work and continually look for ways you can improve your skills or practices – keep in touch with your peers to share best practice. Make sure you know what it is you want your life to be about, and if work is encroaching on that, consider changing jobs or changing your work pattern. Most importantly, communicate to your boss that you're suffering high levels of stress and the effect this is having on you. Ask for his or her suggestions and make a well-founded proposal to rectify the situation, supplying facts and figures. Other than that, recognize your limits – never, ever let stress damage your health, but also realize that a bit of stress makes the day go with a zing and helps us focus.

Manage your time by prioritizing your workload using the task prioritization matrix, and understand the difference between the important things and the urgent things. Motivate yourself to reach the deadline by being clear that: 'I have to do this task *because... by* (such a time)... and *why* it's needed by that time is because...'. Ask yourself if you are working on the right thing at the right time in the right way and eliminate procrastination. Organize yourself and your boss so that you are able to meet deadlines by following the e-mail guidelines, using the power of the subconscious to help you be creative and getting rid of your negative gremlins. Stretch your goals, which in turn increase your self-belief and your confidence, and have fun decreasing your stress levels.

Having your time management under control and using visualization techniques to reduce stress mean that you will not suffer from stress-related illnesses and relationship problems. You will therefore experience healthy pressure to energize you to achieve your goals and to-do list and be exhilarated and satisfied.

Each night before you go to sleep, think back over the day's activities, remember what you have managed to get done and congratulate yourself for effective and efficient time management that day. It is a satisfying feeling as you drift off to a contented sleep that you have achieved so much with your time that day.

Practise all the above suggestions and solutions to get your time management and stress levels under control, and enjoy an efficient and effective working day every day.

Organizing meetings and events

06

One of the main roles of an assistant is to organize meetings of all different sizes of groups from two to a thousand or more and for all levels of staff/clients/guests. Meetings are arranged for many different reasons (Table 6.1) and involve internal and/or external national/international attendees. They could be virtual or face-to-face meetings. Some will include activities and entertainment and some will involve PowerPoint slides, flip charts, video conferencing and the like. The meetings could be ones your boss will chair or participate in; they could be team-building events for your company,

TABLE 6.1 Reasons for holding meetings

To inform each other of what is going on and to help build relationships	For problem-solving purposes and decision making
To disseminate the vision of the company	Formal gatherings for consultation
Communication	Launch of a new product
Training, team building, education, entertainment and discussion	Presentation and proposals for new work
Client/business meetings	Seminar/conference

one-to-one meetings (eg for appraisals/interviews), or meetings you hold for your team of assistants. (If you don't already hold meetings for assistants, I suggest you think about putting them in place.)

> An efficiently organized and executed meeting could be critical to your boss's, your company's and your own success!

It is imperative that meetings are not time-wasters. Attendees should leave feeling satisfied that actions are being taken and progress is being made towards positive and constructive outcomes and that objectives are achieved. Meetings are expensive, so it's important to ensure that every person attending and every minute of the meeting add value.

> To make meetings successful they need to be managed before, during and after the meeting.

Before the meeting: prepare and plan!

Appendix 11 (online) provides a comprehensive generic checklist for meetings and events. Details of each task are set out in the sections below.

Need for meeting

Decide whether the meeting is necessary, and be clear about why it is needed – you may need to challenge your boss!

- Could objectives be achieved more effectively through another process?
- Could the meeting be held by video link or webinar?
- Could it just be a telephone call or conference call?
- Is it being held in the right time frame?

Timing and invitations

Do you need more time to invite guests/delegates? (Invitations to events should ideally be sent out at least six to eight weeks prior to the event, if possible, to ensure that you meet attendance targets.)

Define purpose of meeting

- What are your objectives for the meeting and what techniques should be used – eg brainstorming/brain dumping/blue sky/workshop/note taking?
- What are you trying to achieve?
- What decisions need to be made?
- What actions need to be taken?
- Ensure that all attendees understand the purpose of the meeting to achieve an effective and efficient outcome.

Budgeting and booking

Establish whether a budget is needed and, if so, what the budget is.

If required, choose and book an event-management company or enlist the help of colleagues.

Choose and book a suitable meeting room, venue and location. You can use referrals, search on the internet or use a venue-finding agency, whose services are free to you as the hotel pays their commission. Always visit the venue yourself.

Book any break-out room(s) required. Establish whether you would need a registration desk and where it could be situated. Consider the impression you want to give when booking a venue. Do you require a day delegate rate, half-day delegate rate, 24-hour delegate rate? Check for any extra costs that may be charged, for equipment or break-out rooms, water for the tables occupied by delegates and speakers, hire of cloakroom staff/bar staff and so on. Learn to negotiate a good price for the venue, entertainment, speakers, transport and other elements.

Depending on the type of event/meeting you are holding, consider where people are travelling from and think about car-parking availability. You may need to plan and organize travel arrangements, such as the hiring of coaches or limousines, and book taxis, train tickets or flights to facilitate travel to and from the venue and possibly during the event.

Venue

When choosing a venue, consider whether leisure activities will be required, such as a spa, gym or golf course. Types of venues to choose from include:

- your own company's offices;
- clients' offices;
- hotels;
- country house estates;
- convention and exhibition centres;
- important attractions;
- tourist attractions;
- museums;
- theatres;
- university lecture theatres.

Consider whether overnight accommodation is required for speakers/delegates.

Decide what the room layout should be, depending on the event and numbers attending, for example theatre style, cabaret round tables with cloths on them, boardroom style, cabaret half-moon style, open square, U-shape seating or classroom style. Is a top table required? If this is a one-to-one meeting for an appraisal or interview, the room should be set out so that the two chairs are not separated by a table and are at 45° to each other. This reduces any psychological barriers and encourages a successful meeting.

You may require the room to be dressed and themed. This may be something the venue can sort out for you, or if you have an event-management team they can do it. Alternatively you may just want to organize flower centrepieces for each table or candles on mirrors in the centre of the table for a more cost-effective way to dress the room. Ask the venue staff for their suggestions and what they can supply within the cost. Some venues may have their own chair covers and ribbons for the chairs, which can transform a room; otherwise these have to be hired in.

If the location is an outside venue, negotiate the package and discuss all requirements and expectations, including appropriate room size for the number of attendees.

Avoid signing any contract with the venue until you really have to, in case things change. When you have to put your signature on the dotted line, please make sure that you have permission and authority to do so from your boss. Also make sure that you have read and re-read the contract for correct details, numbers, timings and so on. Make sure too that you understand and agree with the 'minimum number of delegates' requirement, because it means that even if you do not have as many delegates as your minimum number you still have to pay for them. Also check cancellation fees and timings, and the latest time and date that you can make your final changes to the meeting. Please note that you should not pay VAT on cancellation charges as you will not have received any service.

Arrange for a deposit to be paid if required.

If you are having a corporate event such as disseminating information to clients, find out who else is using the hotel the same day and for what reason, to avoid any embarrassing clashes.

Entertainment/speakers

Make sure that you have the correct insurance cover when using entertainment such as bands with electronic equipment.

If entertainment or a speaker is required, look for recommendations and referrals from people you know and trust, or go and see them yourself in action in order to ensure a successful event and the satisfaction of all attendees. Send out a briefing note to them before the event so that they know what is required of them.

Equipment

Book any equipment and/or event company for audio-visual equipment, screens, DVD players, digital projectors, simultaneous-translation equipment, microphones, plasma screens and so on. Remember to order a small table to accommodate a laptop and digital projector if you are taking your own. Tables and chairs may need to be hired in. Also check if extension leads are needed and make sure that they are taped to the floor for health and safety.

Find out what equipment people will require you to provide and what they will provide themselves. Assess how much space will be needed for it. Will staging be needed? If so, is it available at the venue or does it need to be bought in? Consider obtaining the speaker's presentation before the event so that you can make sure it works on your equipment and is loaded and ready to go when needed.

Consider whether your meeting/event will require the use of the venue's business centre for fax, photocopier and so on. Will you need broadband access for laptops? Decide whether you will need to use a message board so that delegates can check for messages during breaks and lunch time.

Security

You may need to consider organizing special security arrangements. For example, I once had a power boat and a racing car standing at the entrance to the venue as part of the charity auction prizes. I had to organize a security guard to be there all night to make sure they were safe.

Reception

If you are having identity badges for delegates or need people to register on arrival, make sure that you have organized a registration/reception desk and decide exactly where the table should be located in the venue. It should be as close as possible to the room being used so that you can capture all arrivals.

If you are to be on the reception desk, make sure you know where the ladies and gents toilets are, and the nearest fire exits, so that you are able to direct people as soon as you are asked. Also ask the facilitator of the event to announce where toilets and fire exits are, and find out whether a fire-alarm test is to run on the day you have your meeting so that guests can be informed.

A cloakroom should be available and manned if necessary (even in summer; attendees may have luggage and briefcases they wish to store while in the meeting).

Signage

Ensure that there is clear signage for your meetings so that attendees can easily find their way to the room, and that all logos, noticeboards and banners are provided. If necessary, you may want to place people in the foyer of a hotel or venue to direct people (if the staff of the venue are not available for this).

Refreshments

Depending on the length and timing of the meeting, ensure that sufficient and appropriate refreshments/meals are ordered and stipulate the times they are to be served. Also decide whether any meal should be a hot or cold buffet or sit-down meal (à la carte or set menu). Decide whether the meal should be taken in a private dining area, as a finger buffet in the conference room or in the venue's dining room.

Does the venue have its own caterers or do you have to bring caterers in? If it is a formal dinner for a large group, I strongly suggest that you ask for a 'taster' session of the food so that you can make an informed choice. Chefs expect you to do this. Ascertain any dietary requirements and send them in written format to the venue to confirm your requirements. Always ensure that these are understood by the venue, as there are many intolerances/allergies to food as well as religious requirements to be considered. You may have to order kosher or halal food from an outside company, including plates and cutlery.

Attendance

Attendance should be restricted to those who are vital to the meeting, those who have to be there for training or information and so on, and those with essential information or expertise.

Limit or preferably eliminate those who feel they ought to be there if they do not fit the above criteria.

Agenda

Send the agenda out to all delegates before the meeting and ask for any comments/additions to the agenda. Make sure that participants know what is expected of them, and send out well in advance any documents they may need to read/digest/action before the meeting. Make amendments to the agenda if necessary when feedback is received.

Include only those items relevant to the purpose of the meeting. Ideally you should indicate the time allowed for each item to make sure that the agenda is completed in the allotted time; this also makes everyone aware of the timekeeping, which will help the meeting to run smoothly and effectively. Prioritize your agenda items and sort them in order of importance (grouping related items together), in case not all items are discussed owing to unforeseen circumstances, interruptions and possibly bad timekeeping.

If you are organizing a committee meeting, you should send out the minutes of the last meeting as a reminder (the minutes should also have been sent out shortly after the last meeting).

Documentation for the meeting

The invitation, agenda and relevant documentation should be circulated in good time before the meeting. Attendees can be asked to print the documentation off and bring it when they attend, or they can be told that copies will be provided at the meeting.

Collate documents and information relevant to the agenda items. If they are lengthy, they can be summarized. Some documents may only be required by the chairperson, but others may need photocopying for distribution to the attendees.

The invitation should ask about any dietary requirements if food is to be included in the meeting/event. It should also include: location, start and finish times, and any preparation to be done by the attendees (eg reading of any material).

If the meeting is an internal one, it is possible to post agendas and useful meeting notes on a dedicated company intranet web page for everyone to access. This may cut down the time needed for the meeting if the attendees review any documentation beforehand and act on any necessary points. Then the meeting can be used to get down to further business immediately.

Consider whether you need to send out any flyers to advertise the event, press releases, booking forms, invitation cards and so on, and whether you need to provide freepost code or prepaid envelopes for replies. Do you need any printing done for the advertising and/or handouts/delegate packs, including DVDs for advertising, radio or TV commercials and so on? If you need to produce a DVD of the event, book an appropriate specialist company to do this.

You may need to book/organize rehearsal and set-up time for the venue and the people involved. In that case, it may be necessary to book the venue for the morning, afternoon or evening before the event.

Once an invitation has been sent out, you need to collate replies and acceptances and acknowledge receipt, stating that more information/joining instructions will be sent out nearer the time.

It is important to send out, say a week or two before the event, a 'joining instruction' by e-mail or letter confirming that you are expecting the attendees, giving the time and location (include a map for their convenience), the best place to park and so on. If necessary, do not forget to provide and organize a programme for the persons accompanying the participants if spouses/partners are invited to some or all of the event. This all acts as a reminder as well as being helpful to the attendees. If for any reason they cannot now make it, they can let you know so that you can make alternative arrangements; for instance, you may have a reserve list of people wanting to attend.

Prepare an evaluation sheet to give to delegates at the end of the event/ meeting if appropriate, to include feedback on the administration, the venue, the food, the location, the parking, the content of the event/speakers/ entertainment and so on.

Events team

You may need to put an events team together, so think about the skills and technical ability they can bring: social skills for the registration desk, IT skills for equipment and so on. Make them aware of the objectives of the event/meeting and brief them in advance, possibly meeting a couple of times before the event.

Create and circulate an events schedule for all those involved in helping you put the event together, and re-send it when changes are made.

Training

You may need training in managing the events team when coordinating and running the event if you are doing it yourself. You can use simple Word documents to help you organize your event/meetings, Gantt charts or sophisticated computer programs. You may also need training in the latter.

Flexibility

Always be prepared, for your own peace of mind, and always be ready to accept that changes will happen the closer you get to the event. It is inevitable that a minority of people will drop out for reasons beyond anyone's control. It is better to accept this fact – take it in your stride and deal with it calmly and efficiently – than to let yourself get agitated or upset. It is just one aspect of organizing events and meetings that will always happen and it is quite normal to have a few 'no-shows'.

> Problems may occur when organizing events but it is how you deal with those problems that make you an exceptional assistant.
> Being in control is 10 per cent what happens to you, and 90 per cent how you respond to it!

During the meeting/event

- Arrive early and set up the room (for a big event this could have been done the day before).

- Debrief anyone involved in helping you organize the event.

- Have your checklist ready and make sure that everything is as you have planned, including making sure that the delegate handouts are in place.

- Make sure the room is set out as planned and that there are enough chairs with a few spare.

- Register people to the event/meeting and give out name badges if appropriate.

- Check the temperature of the room and regulate if necessary.

- Adhere to programme timings for start, breaks, meals and finish.

- Usher in any late arrivals and try to leave some room for them at the back so that they can 'sneak' in.

- Be on hand throughout the whole meeting/event for any unforeseen problems and be ready to solve them.

- If there are any distracting/disturbing noises (perhaps from kitchens or building work, or attendees forgetting to turn their phones off), put an immediate stop to them.

- At the end of the meeting, collect any name badges and completed evaluation sheets, and distribute goodie bags or handouts as appropriate.

- If car-parking tokens are required or car-parking tickets need to be stamped for attendees to get out of the car park, make sure that they are aware they need to do this.

- Thank them for coming and say goodbye.

See Chapter 11 on 'Confident minute-taking' to learn how to take the minutes of any meeting, and how you should work with the chairperson.

After the meeting: evaluate

- Summarize the evaluation sheets and act on any outstanding points. Keep the sheets as guidance for future events.

- Send out any minutes and action points and make sure that they are completed.

Successful meetings and events are organized by an assistant who understands that there are different purposes and types of meeting and event, with specific formats and objectives for each. You need to organize them with careful planning and preparation, stated objectives and a detailed agenda in collaboration with the 'owner' of the meeting/event.

Remember that technology can provide effective tools to make the best use of meeting times and for scheduling, sharing information and even eliminating the need to have face-to-face meetings. Find out what works for you, your boss, your company and the specific meeting or event you are organizing and put them in place.

Having a strategy for before, during and after meetings ensures well-organized meetings with all points covered, enabling communication. It also ensures less anxiety for you, your boss and the attendees. Use the above tips together with Appendix 11 and information in Chapter 11 on minute-taking and work with the chairperson. This will not only ensure successful organization of meetings and events, but it will also help you to develop an effective working relationship with your boss.

07

Presentations

From the moment we are born our brains start working, and they do not stop until we stand up to give our first presentation. People have three main fears:

- the fear of dying;
- the fear of presenting;
- the fear of dying while presenting!

The more you practise the easier it gets, and assistants have the opportunity to give presentations on various occasions: company secretarial/assistant team meetings, reporting back to the company board and at conferences to help other secretaries, among others. You may want to be empowered by dealing with work projects, such as teaching new managers how to interact with their assistants or teaching ergonomics to anyone who uses a computer at a desk. You can take opportunities to present at internal as well as external networking meetings, which may mean that you have to get out of your comfort zone but will result in the satisfaction of learning a new skill that you can add to your CV.

This chapter will give you tips for success. Alternatively, you can use it to help your boss put together an efficient and effective presentation and to present effectively.

Performing in front of others can be daunting and it is perfectly normal to feel nervous. In fact, even the most experienced presenters feel a little nervous just before they start speaking, but this is good; it produces adrenalin which helps to increase your energy, resulting in an energized and better presentation. Public speaking can be fun and hugely satisfying. Once you have enjoyed giving a presentation, or even part of one, your self-confidence will grow and you'll want to do it again.

Most probably you have one or two of the following symptoms of nervousness:

- fast heartbeat;
- dry throat;
- shaky knees;
- sweaty palms;
- shaky hands;
- nausea.

There are tools and techniques to help you channel your adrenalin in the right direction to help you present to the best of your ability. What you do about your nerves is crucial. Physical and vocal exercises/warm-ups before presenting are extremely effective at alleviating stress and also help us to be more expressive and able to project our voices.

Exercises to reduce tension

Reducing tension in neck and shoulders

Tension can easily build up in the neck and shoulders. A technique to help you is to exercise before you make a presentation. Concentrating on a minute or two of physical exercise will not only get rid of discomfort but can also energize you and help put you in a better frame of mind to give your best. Find a quiet place where you can be alone for a minute or two.

Sit up straight and slowly move your head to your left, back to the centre, over to the right and back to the centre. Then move your head up and back and then slowly down to your chest. Repeat these several times, keeping all movements steady and slow, and the routine will help to release tension in your neck and shoulders.

Breathing exercises

Take several deep breaths to get the oxygen circulating around your body.

The technique of alternate nostril breathing can help to balance the nervous system. Clear your nostrils by breathing in and out quickly several times in a row. Next, place your hand so you can use the thumb to close one nostril and your ring finger to close the other. Begin by inhaling through both nostrils. Then breathe out through one nostril while blocking the other, and switch and breathe in through the other nostril. After three complete breaths, exhale without switching sides, and do three more breaths.

After this you will be in a better frame of mind to give your best and enjoy your presentation.

Vocal exercises

Vocal exercises help to open up your vocal cords to allow you to project your voice and extend the range of pitch as well as alleviating tension. One such exercise is to screech with a high-pitched 'eeeeeeek'.

Principles for preparing your presentation

Successful presenting consists of three elements:

- *Content*: The presentation should be packed with practical and easy-to-remember information. Inject enthusiasm about the topic into your presentation through your voice and body language. Ask the audience questions so that they have to keep awake, think and answer – delegates like to be involved. Include exercises where they can work together and start to bond with each other – this is particularly good when working with teams. Keep your presentation to the point and practise it to make sure that it lasts the length of time you are allotted to speak, taking into consideration question and answer time if appropriate. Always remember that you may miss out something you intended to say, but the audience will never know that you missed it out, so don't worry about it. Tell short stories to bring your presentation to life (these may be humorous) but be careful about telling jokes as they can seem out of place.

- *Confidence*: Remember that some people get nervous in audiences too. You can put them at their ease by showing with your body language that you are confident of your ability; let them realize that they will enjoy the forthcoming presentation. Knowing that you have information to share that is valuable for others also gives you confidence and satisfaction. (Read Chapter 3 for more on confidence building.) Confidence will come with practice and with performing and being successful.

- *Practice*: It is extremely important to write your presentation and practise, practise, practise until you can present with ease. You should practise to hear, feel and experience the words you use until it sounds natural and comfortable. Video yourself and watch it back and also ask friends to listen to you and critique you to help you get it right. You need to familiarize yourself with the content and make sure it flows right and in a logical order. You should also practise the intonation, body language, eye contact etc.

If you find yourself 'hmmming' and 'errring', begin to realize when you do it and pause instead, putting in a mental full stop, then breathe and start again. Pauses are often good to give the audience time to think about what you have just said and can have more impact on what you are about to say as they wait with bated breath. Also, your voice will have more energy for having stopped and restarted.

Being comfortable with silence can be a powerful tool!

The second way of getting a flow is to build up for yourself a stack of 'link' words and phrases which take you and your audience to the next thought/comment/section without any umms. For example: 'So, what happened next?', 'That leads me nicely on to...', 'You might be asking...', etc.

Benjamin Franklin said: 'The best ad hoc speech I have given is the one I prepared the most.'

Remember that verbal and non-verbal communication work together to convey a message. You can use non-verbal signals and gestures to reinforce and support what you are saying, especially when presenting. You project credibility through your body language, voice quality, gestures, eyes and posture. The audience will remember only 7 per cent of the words you say; 93 per cent of what they will remember is your attitude, tone of voice and your physical presentation skills.

Once you know your presentation thoroughly, you then have to concentrate on how to give it in the most effective and memorable way you can. Make a connection with the audience by eye contact and draw them into the message you wish to give by making it alive and interesting. Then the audience will be listening to every word and waiting to hear what you have to say next. You can use your experiences and anecdotes to help people remember the points you are making. You can also use a mnemonic to link

FIGURE 7.1 Mnemonic for active listening

L **Look and sound interested –**
Listen with eyes, ears and heart!

I **Information**
'Seek first to understand and then be understood'

S **Silence yourself**
Take a breath, relax and smile

T **Test understanding**
Tell me what you think I said and what you think I meant

E **Evaluate the message**
Including body language, look for congruency

N **Note-taking**
Always have your notepad with you and write everything down

Copyright Sue France Training 2012

key messages together and help retention; Figure 7.1 gives an example of a mnemonic for active listening.

If you want to stand out from the crowd and deliver a truly powerful presentation, you have to look at it from the perspective of your audience and see, hear, feel the presentation from their point of view, understanding their wants and needs. Sometimes this could be achieved by sending out a questionnaire before the presentation so that you can deliver their exact requirements. Think about what the audience might already know and already have experienced, and never underestimate the audience's intelligence or overestimate their knowledge. You should realize and acknowledge that some of what you are saying may not be entirely new to them, but it does act as a reminder. Try to talk the same language as them, anticipate any questions and use influencing skills to match their personalities.

Strategy

When writing a presentation, you should use the 'Tell–Show–Tell' principle:

1 Tell them what you are going to show them – the objectives of the presentation.

2 Show them what you told them you are going to show them – do as you said.

3 Tell them what you showed them – reiterate what they have learnt.

You can use the structure of having a beginning, middle and end to your presentation. Alternatively, you can use past, present and future for telling your 'story'. If you use past, present and future then you can use the appropriate space: when speaking about the past you should stand to the left of the stage (left from the delegates' point of view). When speaking about the present you should speak from the centre of the stage and when speaking about the future you should present from the right of the stage. In NLP terms, looking over to the left is the past and remembering and looking over to the right is the future.

Handouts

You may need to prepare handouts for the presentation. These could be copies of your PowerPoint presentation, printed three slides to a page, with a space for the delegates to write notes next to each slide. Handouts could serve just as a reminder after the presentation (remembering that listeners will remember only 7 per cent of the words spoken unless they write notes). It may sometimes be appropriate to ask the delegates not to look at the printed handout during the presentation if you don't want them to know what is coming on the next slide or to read through the material before you deliver it.

Before the presentation

Make sure that you familiarize yourself with the room where you will present and that everything is the way you want it to be. Taking account of the reason for the meeting, you should decide on how you want the room set up: theatre style, boardroom style, horseshoe shape, half cabaret style and so on. Get a 'feel' for the room. Whether you are using a microphone or not, practise speaking and ask someone to stand at the back and check that they can hear you clearly, and make sure that the microphone works properly.

Affirmations

Use affirmations to convince yourself that you are going to give a brilliant presentation. Visualize yourself at the end of it and imagine everyone clapping and smiling and telling you what a really interesting and information-packed presentation you gave. This is similar to the visualization technique that sportspeople use to gain their Olympic medals.

Dress

Make sure that you dress appropriately. Being smart, well dressed and well presented – taking into account your hair, shoes, make-up (for women) and attire – will give you confidence and an air of authority.

During the presentation

It is preferable not to use a lectern as this puts a barrier between you and the audience. However, in order to remain looking forward when giving a PowerPoint presentation, you could have a laptop in front of you as well as having the presentation projected on to the screen behind you. This means that you can keep your face towards the delegates at all times and you can use the slides on the laptop as prompts. Try not to use prompt cards; you should know your material.

Have a glass of water close by in case your throat gets slightly dry through talking, but do not use sparkling water as this can make you belch.

Eye contact

When presenting you should try to keep eye contact with each delegate for about five seconds, or until a message is completed. The benefits of good eye contact are:

- You will make a connection with each person and they will feel included and involved.

- You encourage the audience to participate.

- You appear more in control, and less nervous or uncertain.

- You will establish a two-way communication and you can watch the delegates' body language to establish whether they are confused, bored or needing further explanation. However, please note that you should not take it personally if you see someone falling asleep as you don't know what is going on in their lives – they could have been up all night looking after a baby.

You should never:

- hold your written notes and read from them;
- look over the heads of the participants;
- gaze out of windows;
- stare too long in one direction or at one participant – it is intimidating for them and you appear to be discounting everyone else.

Voice quality

Be aware, at the beginning of your presentation, that your audience need time to get used to your voice, your accent, the phrases you use. As you start to speak they are weighing you up by looking at what you are wearing, the way you have your hair, they may be thinking about a conversation they have just had or a meeting they have attended or thinking about the lighting or heating in the room and whether they like sitting where they are etc. Therefore you should start by speaking slowly and enunciating clearly to engage their minds and bodies. You should also ask them to let you know if for any reason they are not following you or cannot understand you, especially if the audience's mother tongue is not yours. You will feel more in control and they will be grateful. Continue to watch their body language to make sure that they are listening as well as understanding.

It may be necessary to have a microphone to make sure that you are heard by everyone, depending on the numbers in the room, the acoustics and the volume of your voice. Everyone needs to be able to hear you well, so you have to project your voice to the back of the room. Your voice should not be monotonous as it would be boring to listen to and you will appear unenergetic and lacking in confidence.

To help project your voice you need to ensure that you breathe normally. The audience will hear enthusiasm and commitment. Always remember to look forward; do not keep looking around at the screen as your voice will be directed away from the delegates.

Be particularly careful not to drop your voice at the end of sentences or the delegates will miss what you are saying. However, if you sometimes speak slowly and in a low tone you will be perceived as being credible and powerful.

Speaking pace

Make sure that you speak at a pace that is easily heard and understood by everyone, taking extra care if you have people in the audience whose mother tongue is not the same as the language you are speaking. Use pauses to make a point, telling your audience what is important to remember. The more complex or important the point, the more slowly you should speak, and you can even repeat the sentence to emphasize.

Pitch

Your pitch is affected by your breathing. If your breathing is shallow and nervous, when you start to speak you will sound squeaky, shaky or very low. Practise deep breathing before you enter the room.

Speak clearly and concisely

Speaking clearly and pronouncing your words properly will be much appreciated by the delegates as they will not have to strain to understand you.

Visual aids

DVDs

If you are going to show a DVD or part of one, you must test it before the event to make sure it works properly.

Flip charts

You can use flip charts to document ideas taken from the delegates, for example when brainstorming an issue. You should use thick marker pens in dark colours so that they can be seen clearly from the back of the room. Your handwriting should be legible and of a size that can be seen easily by everyone. It is best practice to use two different colour marker pens alternately for each bullet point written on the flip chart. If you use more than one sheet and you need the delegates to keep referring back to the completed flip chart, you can tear off the sheet and fix the paper to the walls (using a product that will allow you to remove it later without leaving a mark, and making sure that the venue staff agree this can be done).

You can prepare headings and diagrams on the flip chart before the presentation starts. You can also write reminder notes in very small writing in pencil that are not visible to the audience but act as a reminder to you.

When recording participants' responses, use their actual words rather than your own interpretation of what you think they meant – certainly never change the meaning and do acknowledge their thoughts and ideas. This gives them a sense of ownership and reinforces their active participation.

If you are no longer using the flip chart and do not want the delegates to keep looking at what has been written, remember to turn it over to show a blank piece of paper before you move on to the next part of the presentation.

PowerPoint presentations

The advantages of PowerPoint presentations are:

- They are an *aide-mémoire* and are particularly useful for people who process their world visually. (See Chapter 2 for more explanation of this.)
- They show off your technical expertise.
- Your presentation will have a professional appearance.
- You can show one bullet point at a time, use highlights and fading, and make effective transitions.

During the presentation you should use a wireless slide clicker to move your slides on, so that you are not required to stand by your laptop. When you are not referring to a visual, turn off the screen to ensure that the delegates' attention is on you.

Tips for producing PowerPoint presentations

- Font size should be 44 point for headings and 28 point for bullet points.
- Limit the number of fonts (maximum two per slide).
- Use your company branding for your presentation backgrounds.
- Avoid vertical lettering as it is difficult to read.
- Keep it simple and have a maximum of seven bullet points (key words only) to each slide – these are only prompts for you to expand upon.
- Practise using the equipment, making sure that it all works and it is clear on the screen (not blurred). Check for any glare on the screen and adjust lighting/focus accordingly.
- Where appropriate, use cartoons, symbols, graphs and pictures to illustrate a message instead of using words.

Posture, movement and space

As a general rule, stand with feet hip-width apart and sometimes with one foot slightly back, with your arms slightly away from your body and palms facing towards the audience. Never fold your arms, put your hands in your pockets or stand with arms behind your back. You can move around to add variety to the presentation but it is advised that you position yourself in the middle of the available space, at the front and slightly to the right of the room if possible (equidistant from the furniture around you). It has been shown that you can influence your audience better when they have to look to their right towards you (because looking over to the right is the future and creativity).

Remember always to speak to the group and not turn round to the screen or speak towards the flip chart.

Ending the presentation

Summarize the key facts of your presentation and leave some time at the end for questions. You may take questions throughout the presentation if you choose, but the audience may be asking about points that will be covered as a matter of course as you proceed through the presentation.

Always finish on time and adhere to any agenda timings.

Evaluation

Always evaluate your presentation by gaining feedback from the audience. Give out an evaluation sheet and at the end of your presentation ask the delegates to complete it while they are there so that you can collect the sheets (you may never receive any feedback if they say they will post/e-mail/fax it to you). If you pay attention to their comments and revise your presentation accordingly and appropriately, you will learn how to give the best presentation you possibly can.

 Remember: Giving presentations can be fun and tremendously satisfying!

Effective presenters adopt an authoritative and powerful posture and position. How we use our body language, eye contact and stance commands attention before we even start to speak. You want to engage with the audience, understanding their needs and wants, and focus their attention. The audience want certainty that you will deliver what has been advertised, they want to understand why you should be speaking to them and they want to see confidence in your ability.

Once you've enjoyed giving a presentation, or even part of one, your self-confidence will grow. The more you practise the better you will get, and the more you will enjoy and look forward to giving presentations. Give yourself the best chance by using the above tips.

08

Ergonomics: your health and safety

Ergonomics is the science that addresses people's performance and well-being in relation to their job, equipment and environment.

Failure to observe ergonomic principles may have serious repercussions, not only for individuals, who could develop illnesses such as repetitive strain injury, but for whole organizations. Organizations can be held responsible if they do not enforce ergonomic principles, or at the very least they may suffer a high level of sickness absence.

Stress in the workplace can be caused by emotional demands (eg job design, supervision, colleagues), physical demands (eg muscular or visual strain) or environmental demands (eg temperature, noise, air quality) that cause physical or mental tension. Please see Chapter 5 for more information on dealing with emotional stress. This chapter will deal with muscular, visual and environmental aspects.

The work station

Your work station should be ergonomically designed so that it is laid out in the best way to help with your time management.

Apply work zone principles

A work zone is the area in which your equipment and materials are located at your work station. Arrange your work zone to suit the way you work and the tasks you do.

There are three zones, defined by the distance from your usual seated or standing position: the primary zone, the secondary zone and the reference zone.

The primary zone

The primary zone is closest to you and is for equipment and materials used most frequently or for the longest period of time, for example your phone, pad and pen, keyboard, mouse, dictaphone, document holder or computer screen.

Position the keyboard and mouse so that you can keep your elbows close to your body to stop any strain on the back of your neck and arms.

Place your phone on the opposite side to your dominant hand. If you are right-handed your phone should be on your left-hand side and a pad and pen should be to your right. This enables you to pick the handset up easily and quickly with your left hand, leaving your right hand free to quickly find your pen and pad to write messages without twisting your body.

If you use a document holder, any documents that you wish to copy from should be on the side of your dominant eye. The documents should be at eye level, as should the screen, so that you are not hanging your head, which could lead to neck ache and headaches.

How to find out which is your dominant eye:

1 Hold your arms straight out in front of you and put your right-hand fingers over the top of your left-hand fingers; your right-hand thumb should overlap your left-hand thumb, with both thumbs pointing downwards, leaving a circular gap between the crux of your thumbs and your hands (just a bit bigger than a £2 coin or half dollar) that you can look through.

2 Hold your hands out straight in front of you and look through the hole between them with both eyes open. Focus on an object around six feet or more away; this could be, for example, a light switch on the wall. You should focus on the light switch and be able to see it clearly.

3 Keep your head and hands perfectly still, and focus on the light switch with both eyes open. Then close your left eye – if you can still see the object clearly, mentally note that.

4 Still keeping your arms and head in the same place, open both eyes and make sure that you can see the object clearly with both eyes

open. Then close your right eye and see if you can still see the object clearly, and mentally note that.

If you can see the object through the hole made by your hands and thumbs when you close your left eye, then you are right-eye dominant. If you can see the object through the hole when you close your right eye, then you are left-eye dominant.

Similarly, if you cannot see the object through the hole when you close your left eye, then you are left-eye dominant. If you cannot still see the object through the hole when you close your right eye, then you are right-eye dominant.

In other words, the eye that keeps the object in the centre of the circle is dominant.

It is quite rare, but some people may be able to see the object whether they close their right or left eye, meaning that they don't have a dominant eye – but so far I've never met any of these people.

The document holder, then, should be placed on the side of your dominant eye. It may take a few days to feel comfortable with this but it will soon feel much better than when you had the document holder on the wrong side. (You may feel more comfortable immediately, or you may already have the document on the correct side for you just because it felt better there – owing to your dominant eye.) Your brain can coordinate better with your eyes and fingers when typing when documents are placed on the side of your dominant eye and I believe it actually makes you quicker.

The secondary zone

The secondary zone is for items you need to reach or see on a daily basis but for shorter periods of time: your calculator, files you frequently need and so on.

The reference zone

The reference zone is the area for items you use occasionally and usually have to move from your normal position to access: folders used less frequently, scanner, photocopier and so on.

- Position materials to minimize twisting and bending.
- Position heavy manuals on shelves or surfaces that you can reach without stretching high or far from your body.

A tidy desk leads to a tidy mind

Keep your desk tidy and be able to find files, folders and information quickly and easily. To help clear your desk of papers:

- Put work to be dealt with today in the pending tray.
- Delegate work off your desk to someone else.
- Send it to archive storage.
- File it away in the current filing system.
- File it in the reminder system.
- Dump it in the bin.

Clear out items from underneath your desk to allow adequate room to move your legs. Make sure that you don't have any loose wires or leads under your desk.

Your screen

Your screen should be at right angles to a window so that the glare from the sun does not shine on it. The window should never be behind you. Ideally the top of the screen should be at eye level, although if you are using a laptop this may not be possible unless you use a separate keyboard.

Clean the screen regularly and adjust the focus, brightness and contrast controls if appropriate.

Desk height

Your desk should be at a height where, if you hang your arms down by your sides and bend your elbows so that your arms are bent at right angles in front of you, your hands are level with the desk top.

If your desk height cannot be changed, you should lower or raise your chair. Also move it so that you are able to reach the keyboard with your upper arm still kept close to your body.

Chair

If adjusting your chair height results in your feet being off the ground, you need to use a footstool. Your legs should be bent at the knees and again should be at a 90° angle, with your feet resting comfortably on the floor or stool.

Your chair backrest should be adjusted so that you have support in the small of your back – the lumbar region (lower back). This may mean that you need to use a cushion to make sure that your back is supported properly. To find the lumbar region that requires supporting, reach behind your back and place your little finger at waist height, then spread and flatten your hand upward from your waist. The area between your thumb and little finger is the area of your lumbar curve that needs supporting.

Principles of posture

Pay careful attention to the positioning of your head, neck and spine, arms and wrists, pelvis and thighs, and feet. Find the position that places the least stress on your musculoskeletal system.

The spine has three natural curves: one at the neck (the cervical area) and two in the back (the thoracic and lumbar areas). The spine is balanced when these curves are maintained.

When you lean forward, the back muscles are used to support your head. If they are used too much in this way, they will eventually become stiff and tight. This is why we need to sit upright with our heads straight and not leaning forward. Hence the need for the screen to be at eye level (when you are sitting up straight).

Head

Your head should be comfortably aligned so that its support comes from the spine, not from neck and shoulder muscles. You also need to move your head frequently. If you do not follow these guidelines your neck and shoulder muscles remain contracted and the likelihood of headache and fatigue is increased.

Neck/spine

Your neck and spine should be fairly straight or slightly reclining, with the lumbar region (lower back) supported. This region is the focal point for many back problems because it carries the weight of the body and provides the leverage for twisting and bending. Lower back muscles are frequent areas of tension. Tucking in your abdomen automatically helps support your spine and back muscles.

Arms/wrists

Your upper arm should be parallel to your body. Your lower arm should be at approximately a 90° angle, depending on the height of your keyboard surface. The position of your arms should not cause unnecessary stress and fatigue on the forearm, neck and shoulder muscles.

Wrists should be on an even line with the forearm. A bend either up or down may increase pressure on the median nerve and muscles involved in keying or handling other equipment.

I advise that you use a gel pad to rest your wrist on – especially the wrist that uses the mouse. If you rest your wrist on a hard surface you could eventually suffer from carpel tunnel syndrome caused by constant pressure, and you will then require an operation on your wrist.

Pelvis/thighs

Thighs should extend at a 90° angle and the lower legs should be vertical as this position ensures that blood flow in your legs is not diminished by pressure on the back of the legs from the chair.

Feet

Feet should be placed flat on the floor with your legs positioned as described above. If necessary use a footrest to achieve the recommended alignment, maximum blood circulation and muscle relaxation.

Your keyboard

Your keyboard should not be too far away from the edge of your desk; when you have bent your arms you should still be able to reach the keyboard while keeping your upper arms close to your body. You should not be leaning forward with your arms outstretched when using the keyboard. You are most likely to end up with headaches, backache and neck pain in this position and therefore be less effective and less productive.

Once you have made your work area/station ergonomically correct, you will find that you are able to deal with all problems more efficiently and quickly. Your energy levels will increase and physical stress will diminish.

Ergonomic health breaks

There is a strong correlation between fatigue and performance. By controlling fatigue you can prevent musculoskeletal discomfort, maintain mental alertness and maximize performance.

You should take regular breaks away from your screen, which could be from 30 seconds to three minutes every one or two hours. This is a preventive measure to counteract physical symptoms such as headache, visual fatigue and eye strain, neck/shoulder/back pain and overall tiredness. When fatigue is reduced, efficiency rises and the result is an increase in productivity.

Visual strategies

Take your eyes off the screen regularly, either by taking breaks or by alternating your jobs and doing some work that does not require looking at the screen.

You should have regular eye tests every two years.

Regularly look away from the screen and into natural daylight – a good excuse to look out of the window and daydream!

Yawn and blink intentionally occasionally. Yawning is an automatic response that indicates and remedies a craving for oxygen; by increasing oxygen circulation, it relaxes and energizes your body. It also lubricates your eyes, an important benefit while doing close-up work. You may yawn automatically when you see someone else yawning, or can do it intentionally by dropping your jaw line and inhaling. Blinking also helps keep the eyes moist; blinks should be light, quick and effortless – remind yourself to blink when doing close-up work of any kind.

Exercises

It is good to exercise throughout the day to make sure that your body remains stress free and full of energy, and to help prevent repetitive strain injury such as carpel tunnel syndrome. Below are some easy desk exercises:

- *Neck and shoulders.* Sit up straight and slowly move your head to your left, then back to the centre, over to the right and back to the centre. Then slowly move your head up and back and then down to your chest. Repeat these several times to release tension in your neck and shoulders.

- *Computer crunches*. Sit up straight with your feet flat on the floor. Perform a simple pelvic tilt by pressing the lower back into the chair as you contract the abdominal muscles and hold for a few seconds. Relax and then repeat 10–20 times.

- *Bum squeezes*. To tighten your buttocks, sit up straight with your feet flat on the floor. Once again perform a simple pelvic tilt by pressing the lower back into the chair and concentrate on contracting the buttocks. Hold the pose for a few seconds, relax and repeat 10–20 times.

- *Sitting leg extensions*. To work the front of your leg, sit up straight with your feet flat on the floor. Lift and extend the lower right leg with the toes pointed up until the leg is straight, then squeeze the upper leg. Hold for one second, lower the leg and repeat with the left leg. Repeat 10–20 times with each leg.

- *Sitting calf extension*. To tone your calf muscles, sit up straight with your feet around 12 inches or 30 cm apart. Place the weight of your legs on the front or balls of your feet. Slowly lift your heels, toes still touching the floor, squeeze the calf, hold for one second and relax. Repeat 10–20 times.

- *Standing leg curl*. Exercise the upper rear of your leg while reading an e-mail. Stand facing your chair. Lift the right foot off the floor towards the buttocks and hold for one second. Lower the leg and repeat to complete a full set. Do the same for the left leg. Repeat with each leg 10–20 times.

- *Biceps curl*. Keep two 500 ml bottles of water on your desk to use instead of dumbbells. Sit up straight with your feet flat on the floor. Hold the bottles in your palms facing your body. Bend your arm at the elbow while turning your wrists outwards until your palms are facing the ceiling. Lift the bottle towards the shoulder without moving your upper arm. Stop when the bottle meets your shoulder and hold for one second. Lower and repeat 10–20 times with each arm.

- *Triceps extensions*. Sit up straight with your feet flat on the floor. With your right hand raise a bottle of water over your head until your arm is almost straight. Slowly bend your elbow, lowering the weight until your arm forms a 90° angle behind your head. Then extend your elbow until it is slightly bent at the top position. Do not allow the bottle to touch your head or neck area. Lower and repeat.

- *Forward arm circles.* To work your shoulders, sit up straight with your feet flat on the floor and arms extended out at your side. Slowly circle your arms forwards, controlling the movements and focusing on the shoulder muscles.

- *Reverse arm circles.* Sit up straight with your feet flat on the floor and arms extended out at your side. Slowly circle your arms backwards. Control the movements and remember to focus on the shoulder muscles.

- *Stretch.* Stretching is very important and is a great way to de-stress. Begin with your neck, then stretch the shoulders, arms, fingers and then finally your legs.

Ergonomic work stations will increase your health, comfort and safety in the office and will prevent aches and pains in the wrists, shoulders, head, legs and back, reducing stress and thereby improving output and productivity.

Networking

09

What is networking?

Networking can either be face to face or via social media and virtually (see Chapter 12 for more about social media). However you choose to network, it involves getting to know people and developing relationships both inside and outside the organization. Networking is about helping others and receiving help. It's about sharing knowledge. Internally you need to network with all levels of staff, fellow assistants and different divisions such as Information Technology, Procurement, Accounts and Catering. Networking is about giving without obligation, exchanging business cards or telephone numbers/e-mail addresses, working together for a mutual benefit.

> *"Building a strong information network is essential for assistants, adding another dimension to their already strong professional skill set. Networking and forming the right connections will help you position yourself as a hub of information and knowing the right people can get things done. Being a well-connected personal/executive assistant has become an essential part of this role and these are the most sought after for supporting senior executives in organizations, globally."*
> (Warsha Joshi, managing director of Platinum PA Club, Dubai)

The principle of networking is to know–like–trust.

To show people you care, to help build relationships and to establish rapport and trust, you should consider what you have to offer to the people in your network, such as special skills, information, experience and knowledge (known as 'WIIFO' – 'what's in it for others'). You should then ask yourself what you might need help with (known as 'WIIFM' – 'what's in it for me'). Networking is about listening and sharing knowledge and helping each other to achieve your respective goals. Little things such as sharing a useful website link or answering a question in your area of expertise are ways to add value to the people in your network.

Knowledge is power – but it is more powerful when it is shared.

It's amazing how networking with like-minded people can be so rewarding, not only in terms of business outcomes, saving time and gaining valuable information, but also in personal satisfaction and the feel-good factor that we all get when we help others.

The benefits of networking

"Initiate and develop relationships that can help your boss's profile as well as your own."

(Laurel Herman)

Networking can be used to benefit you in a number of ways; for example, it can gain you access to someone in a position of authority who can help you or offer advice. Similarly, it can let you find help for a project you may be working on, such as fundraising for a charity. Your network is also one of the most powerful tools you can have when you are thinking about changing jobs.

Networking within secretarial organizations such as EUMA gives the individual an opportunity to learn new skills and to practise them in a safe environment. This might mean organizing events, taking on committee roles such as chairperson, public relations officer, treasurer, training and educational officer, and so on. You may never get a chance to try any of these within your daily working environment but with EUMA you have every opportunity to do so.

Belonging to a network also makes it possible to share knowledge and information. It is particularly useful to belong to a network if you are a virtual assistant or a personal/executive assistant working on your own for one person at the top of the company, where you may not have many secretarial colleagues around with whom you can share information.

You can also use networking on a wider scale. When you attend business lunches and networking meetings, either on your own or with your boss, on behalf of your company, you are well placed to develop relationships and find out what the needs of other organizations and companies are. Eventually such networking helps to develop your business.

It is so much easier to communicate and work with people when you have met them in person and started to build a relationship with them. That is much better than just working over the phone, hearing the voice of someone you have never met. Assistants need to feel comfortable and confident about working and speaking with clients, and networking will help to develop that confidence.

When sorting out dates for your boss with another assistant, rather than corresponding via e-mail, it is so much better to pick up the phone sometimes and put a voice to the written communication, which is a step towards building relationships. One step better than that is actually to meet them at networking events.

It is a good idea to develop secretarial networks both within your own company and with the assistants of your clients, which can only benefit yourselves and the companies you work for.

Assistants are often referred to as 'gatekeepers' because they have to be very guarded about whom they allow through to speak to their boss either on the phone or face to face. When assistants network together it helps to break that barrier down, making the assistant network an extremely powerful one; one that bosses should support financially and emotionally.

Where to network

Enlightened bosses who realize the immense benefit of their assistants belonging to a network will support them both financially and emotionally. Some assistants and secretaries pay for themselves as it is so rewarding and excellent value for money. You will find networks in the UK and Europe such as EUMA (**www.euma.org**). Other networks include the Australian Institute for Office Professionals, Australian Office Professionals Association, Association for Office Professionals of South Africa, Association of Administrative Professionals New Zealand Inc, Legal Secretaries International Inc (United States), the International Association of Administrative Professionals (United States), and many more in the UK and most countries around the world.

There are also excellent resources and social media networking facilities on the internet, including Facebook, Twitter, Xing, LinkedIn and many others.

See Chapter 12 on social media for more information about networking on these sites and more.

Please note that it is important to do an internet search in your own name to make sure there is no false information about you out there.

You can increase your online profile by engaging in a variety of online activities which demonstrates your skills, knowledge and expertise, such as:

- Engaging in online discussions either by starting a discussion about a topic that interests you or commenting on a discussion which another person has started.

- Writing articles.

- Helping other online contacts as they are more likely to want to help you when you need assistance in the future.

- Sharing information or an idea.

- Asking for advice on a supplier, a hotel, where the best place is to eat in town etc.

Classify your contacts: as your career progresses, not everyone will be as important to your career, your interests or your business as they are currently. Group your contacts as follows and remember to add to them as you meet new people and review the ones you have as their position may change:

Group A: contacts that are well connected to your target market, and are likely to help you immediately achieve your business or career goals.

Group B: contacts whom you enjoyed meeting, but are unlikely to immediately help you achieve your business or career goals.

Group C: contacts you met, but are very unlikely to help you achieve your business or career goals.

(Nicky Morris, experienced executive assistant)

Volunteer to attend your company's client events and be on the registration table where you can meet and network with the clients – this helps later when you are speaking to them on the phone and can put a face to the name. More than that, it will help you become more familiar with them, which helps relationships between your companies.

Networking internally with your colleagues is just as important as networking with external clients/customers.

The secrets of good networking

You should actively network when you attend training sessions, conferences, exhibitions, social events, work meetings, alumni events, evening classes, the gym or even your office restaurant/canteen – you just never know what you will learn and where it will lead. You also never know just how many connections we all have. It is said that we have approximately 250 contacts each, so imagine the potential when we get chatting together! It is also said that you have to make an average of only six connections to get to anyone in the world you want to talk to. You don't know who knows whom..., who knows who knows whom... or even who knows what... until you get talking and networking.

You need to feel self-confident and have self-esteem to be able to walk into a room full of strangers and start networking – or at least you need to be able to fake it. Look confident and you will feel confident – take on the traits of someone whom you know is confident and eventually it will come naturally. (See Chapter 3 to read more on confidence and self-esteem to help you build your confidence.) Also, it is good to remember that most of the people in the networking room will be feeling uncomfortable about networking, so show them how to do it and put them at their ease.

The reason why we find it hard to walk up to strangers and start talking to them is that we have a negative gremlin lurking in our subconscious that was put there when we were young by our well-intentioned parents who told us 'Don't talk to strangers!' Bring out your positive coach, who will tell you that you are no longer a child nor in any danger from strangers, and that it is good to talk to different people as you never know what you will learn or where it will lead.

Be careful, however. Confidence is about getting the right balance – being overly confident can come across as arrogant and unfriendly. You must portray confidence with a friendly and approachable attitude.

When greeting people, be friendly, approachable and warm. As discussed in Chapter 1, shake their hands firmly but not too hard, and be aware of cultural differences to avoid causing offence. Say your first name slowly and clearly, pause, say your first name again and your last name so that the other person hears it properly. Remember the other person's name – repeat it to yourself in your head to fix it instead of letting it just glide over you. It will be important to remember if you are to introduce him or her to someone else later.

Always remember to smile as it not only brightens up your face but increases serotonin levels and makes you feel happier. Also, smiling is contagious – try smiling at someone and you'll see they will smile right back. If you want to feel happier and dispel any first-time nerves when networking, just smile – try feeling sad with a smile on your face – you can't! But it is important to make it a genuine smile, otherwise it could look more like a grimace.

If people are in the full flow of conversation and you want to join them, just stand slightly back, wait to catch their eye and give them a smile and they will invite you in, or just say 'Do you mind if I join you?' Do not interrupt the conversation in full flow as this is bad mannered and can put people off what they were saying or – even worse – cut them off in a story just as they are about to give the punchline!

Once you have exhausted your conversation and you want to continue networking, you can suggest that you introduce the person you were speaking with to someone else, or that you both should circulate or go and join another group, or simply go your separate ways. Alternatively, you could ask someone else to join you and after a few minutes excuse yourself, saying that you have just seen someone you want to catch up with, and leave them chatting.

Some points to remember when attending events:

- If you have a name badge to wear, always wear it on your right-hand side. When you are shaking hands with someone the right-hand side of your body leans over towards them and they will be able to see your badge more easily.

- Try to arrive early at an event as there will be fewer people then and they will not have had a chance to pair up. Arriving early ensures that people will come over to you when they arrive and are looking for a friendly face to talk to if you smile at them as they walk into the room.

- Look for people who are on their own and they will be pleased you walk up to them. Similarly, when you are talking to someone and there is a clear break in the conversation, if you notice someone on their own invite them over to speak to you.

- If you already know someone in the room and you're not sure who to talk to, then have a word with your acquaintance and see if they can introduce you to someone; try to do the same for other people if you can.

- Never look over the shoulder of the person you are speaking to in order to see who else is in the room. That is bad manners. Give the person your full attention.

- Use visual, auditory and kinaesthetic techniques to help build relationships (see Chapter 2 for more on this).

- Understand and use effective body language techniques. See Chapter 1 for information on making a first impression, matching and mirroring, and building relationships. People make up their mind about people in just two seconds when they first meet them!

- Keep eye contact 80% of the time when talking to someone; you will look more interested in them. Your eyes will naturally look to your left when remembering the past, and to the right when thinking about the future, but just remember to bring your eyes back to the other person's. This is true for many cultures, but you must be aware of cultural differences that need to be taken into consideration with regard to eye contact.

- Once other people have had a chance to speak about themselves you can talk about yourself, but be careful not to bore people – watch their body language for signs and change what you are saying if you need to.

Networking is a two-way process, so help your contacts whenever possible and they will help you – this is the 'law of reciprocation'.

Remembering people's names

When people introduce themselves to you and you don't quite catch their name, ask them to repeat it. If it is an unusual-sounding name you might ask them to spell it for you and comment on what a nice name it is – that will help you to remember it. Use the name yourself as often as possible (without overdoing it!) as that helps you remember it – and helps build on the first impressions you make. Bear in mind that the more often you hear and see the name, the more likely it is to sink in. If the person has a card then make sure you get one, and write any appropriate information that you wish to remember on the card.

After you have left that person's company, repeat the name in your mind several times, which helps to put it in your long-term memory. You can help yourself to remember names by associating them with images of a name or with other people (but a word of warning: be careful with this technique as it has been known to result in a Mr Pearce being called Mr Spear!). If you are particularly keen to remember someone and to remember your conversation because you are going to follow up on something, you might decide to write the name down and make notes.

Some general points

- While networking, always be professional and never gossip, especially about current or former colleagues. Remember that those who gossip to you will gossip about you!

- If you have business cards, remember to have them with you when you go networking externally, and take a pen to write down any notes on the card that may be appropriate – writing down information also makes the other person feel more important.

- Your appearance should be smart and professional, including your grooming as well as your clothes.

- Remember to use active listening skills and to let the other person talk, as you only learn about others by listening – not by talking. Be genuinely interested in what others have to say.

- Ask appropriate questions at the right time – see Chapter 2 on questioning skills and below on what to talk about.

- Always listen for chances to help someone. When it is your turn to speak you can say something like: 'You mentioned that you are looking to join a good secretarial networking group. Well, I know of one that works for me – why don't you take a look at **www.euma.org**?'

- When networking, remember to stand at a 45° angle to people so that you leave a space for someone else to join you. Similarly, when you are looking to join a group, look for an opening. When people are standing face to face, do not interrupt them. If you want to talk to just one of them, you can close any gap and face them straight on, but do not stand in their personal space as it could be perceived as confrontational.

- After a meeting, follow up on any promises/agreements made and keep in regular contact with your network to maintain the relationships.

What to talk about while networking

Get people to talk about themselves by asking them questions. People love to talk about themselves and they will feel they have built a good relationship with you even if they haven't found out that much about you yet.

People also feel good when they help others, so ask them to help you. The more specific you can be, the easier it is for them to do so. For example, start with the phrase: 'Please can you help me – do you know anyone who is an expert in..., can advise me about..., knows who can..., knows about...,' or: 'Can tell me where I can find...' or 'If you were me how would you...?'.

When developing presentations or when out networking, the structure of past, present and future can be followed for topics to be talked about. As we've just mentioned, the best way to build relationships is to ask people questions and show a genuine interest in them. If you cannot think of what to ask, then thinking of the past, present and future scenario will help you. You could ask questions about their past, such as 'Have you always worked where you are now?' 'Who did you work for before and what was it like there?' Then you can ask questions about their current role and also about their thoughts and plans for their future.

In the UK it is common to talk about the weather. However, if you are in a country which is hot most of the time then this topic may not be so interesting.

If you are at a meeting that people have had to travel to, you could talk about the journey – 'How did you travel here today?' 'Did you find us easily?' However, a word of warning here – always talk positively, for example: 'I had plenty of time to read on the way down on the train; it got delayed for half an hour but I knew I was still going to be on time so I enjoyed the extra reading time.' Compare this with someone telling you that they had had a terrible journey, that they had missed the train they were supposed to get and then when they got on the next one there was nowhere to sit and the train got delayed for half an hour, which they could well have done without and so on and on. No one wants to hear a tale of woe or listen to someone moaning – the impression you give when meeting for the first time will stick and people like to spend time with happy, positive people.

Also:

- Talk about your job: what it is you do and what you enjoy about it.

- Talk about holidays and travel. Ask people where they went on their holidays and where they intend to go next, what type of holidays are their favourite and whether they can recommend a good place to go.

- Talk about sports – men in particular like talking about sports and cars.

- Talk about current affairs and what is in the news or most topical at the moment. This is a good reason to keep up with watching the news on the television and reading newspapers and industry magazines.

- Talk about families, although it is advisable not to ask people if they have children as this could be a 'sore' point. If they bring up the subject of children, it is fine to talk about it.

If you don't network, you'll never know what it is like or what you are missing – or what you can get out of it for your self-development and how it might affect your career.

It will increase your skill set and help raise your and your organization's profile as you will be the face of your organization while networking externally.

You will make new friends both socially and for business, and it could make your working life much easier when you know the other assistants personally as well as the other influential members of the organization.

Networking is fun, productive, exciting, worthwhile and important for your continuous self-development.

A chapter to share with your boss

10

This chapter is designed to help bosses and assistants have the most rewarding, satisfying and successful relationships possible. None of us is perfect (bosses or assistants) but we can try to keep our flaws small and to the minimum.

Bosses do get lots of training in their working lives but very few are trained specifically on how to work with their assistants. I receive requests from bosses like:

> I wonder if you could let me know what makes a good assistant. I believe my expectations of my assistant are too low and wonder if you have any hints. Perhaps I am not managing him/her effectively. I would be interested in your advice.

> I have not had an assistant before and not sure how to use one. Can you give me some advice, please?

The most useful advice to bosses and assistants is to communicate constantly with each other so that they understand what each expects of the other and understand each other's boundaries and rules. Communication, understanding, respect for each other, trust and empathy are the only way to build a mutually beneficial and successful boss–assistant relationship.

However, many bosses and assistants find it difficult to get the communication started, especially if there is an issue to be cleared up. This chapter can be used as a tool to open up communications between you and to point you in the right direction to make an effective working relationship.

Communication

If you don't know the rules you won't succeed. The rules come from both the boss and their assistant.

The following are top tips given by bosses to help make the relationship work, taken from their own experience:

- To make the relationship work, the manager needs to be open with the assistant. It cannot work if the boss has secret appointments, secret projects and so on. The assistant also needs to know where the boss is at all times, to know whom he or she is dealing with and what his or her relationship is with them so that, for example, the assistant can make an informed decision as to whether or not to get the boss out of a meeting for a telephone call which the caller says is extremely important.

- Bosses should view it as a partnership working together – that involves respect and understanding each other.

- The boss–assistant relationship should be like a good marriage. There should be mutual respect, trust and understanding, a sense of loyalty and a good sense of humour.

- Communicate – tell the assistant what you are doing, where you are going, which are the key clients or projects at the moment and so on.

- Understand the assistant's preferred work pattern and use that to your advantage, for example whether their most productive times of working are in the morning or the afternoon.

- Spend time getting to know and understand your assistant as a person and be aware of their non-work commitments so that you can give flexibility when required, which will be rewarded in the long term.

- Remember that your assistant will have to have worked with you for a long time to get a deep understanding of your priorities and pressures – so be prepared to really explain your motives, pressures and concerns so that he or she can help you to get the best solutions.

- Let your assistant decide how best to do the things that he or she is skilled at – don't over-instruct, as you'll kill your assistant's initiative and never get to see his or her potential.

- When trying to get out of tricky situations with clients, never lay the blame on assistants for something you know they did not do as you will lose their respect, which could cause an effective working relationship to fail.

- Solicit and be open to constructive feedback from assistants on how they think the relationship is working and if there is anything they can suggest to help make the relationship even better.

- Continually and regularly communicate, whether formally, informally, daily, twice daily, weekly, by phone, in meetings, by text – just keep in touch with each other and up to date with everything that is happening.

- It may take a lot of courage on the secretary's part to approach the boss and say what he or she thinks or feels, so the least the boss can do is to encourage the assistant to communicate; the boss should actively listen, empathize and give serious consideration to what is being said – it's about respecting each other.

- Set aside half an hour each week to sit down and explain not just where you are going next week but also what you are aiming to achieve and why.

- Remember that assistants are not paid nearly as much as their bosses, so be appreciative of how hard they work and be reasonable with your demands.

- Encourage self-development and training needs, support and encourage requests for continuous development in both financial and time terms – it pays off in the end.

What bosses should know to work effectively with their assistants

Empowerment

"Never be limited by your job description. On many occasions throughout my career I have been fortunate to work on some extremely satisfying and interesting projects simply because I initiated an action when I saw a need, had the skill or accepted responsibility for something. As a result I have travelled, met some wonderful people, been responsible for some really interesting projects and have certainly not been limited to the traditional concept of an assistant. This has also resulted in several promotions and been very rewarding financially."

(Liz O'Farrell)

Empower your assistant with project work that can take some work away from you and free up your time to do other things. This would allow development; it makes the job more interesting and satisfying and raises self-esteem and morale.

Bosses should think about what would help to relieve them of pressure and at the same time broaden the experience and skill set of the assistant.

> To the boss: Empower your assistant – encourage his or her potential and lighten your load.

Most bosses want to give their assistants power, authority, decision-making capabilities and control over areas of their jobs. So assistants need to take it – ask for it, demand it and grow with it!

Assistants should take action to obtain empowerment – empowerment is an attitude. If you have the attitude that you are willing to accept empowerment then you will be given it. That has significant effects on your self-esteem and morale as it encourages you not only to continually develop by doing new and different tasks but to be given the permission to formulate your own ideas and follow them through.

For empowerment to happen, an assistant requires **permission, power** and **protection**:

- The boss has to agree and give permission to empower the assistant, although the request can come from a proactive assistant.
- That gives you, as assistant, power to make decisions and then you exercise the power, but you also have to know that if something goes wrong you will be protected by your boss as the overall accountability still lies with him or her.

If permission, power or protection is missing, empowerment cannot occur.

A useful project that an assistant might be empowered to do is developing a workshop and teaching new managers how they should interact with their assistants, explaining what is expected of them and what they should expect of their assistants. This would enable you to influence managers who have never had an assistant before on the best way to develop an efficient and effective working relationship, thereby also helping your fellow assistants.

So all bosses and assistants should think about what projects the assistants could be empowered to do – they may be work related, charity related or business development-type work such as looking after the alumni of the organization.

As an assistant, you should seize the opportunity if and when it arises, and volunteer to take on projects – it will enhance your skills base and your career, you will be respected and appreciated for doing it, you will gain experience and knowledge that you might not have otherwise gained, and it will provide you with new achievements that you can add to your CV.

When taking on a project you should:

- Follow through to a project's end, demonstrating tenacity and persistence in completing the project.
- Give attention to detail. Detail is hugely important, especially if you are organizing an event of any kind.
- Take responsibility for the quality of the finished product.

The law of expectations: communicate your expectations clearly

As the boss, it is important to communicate your expectations to your assistant clearly. When communicating expectations, you should be as specific as possible since ambiguity may cause misunderstanding, mistakes and failure.

Your expectations of people and their expectations of themselves are the key factors in how well people perform at work:

- Bosses have expectations of the assistants who work for them and communicate these expectations consciously and subconsciously.
- Assistants consciously and subconsciously pick up on their bosses' expectations.
- Assistants perform in ways that are consistent with the expectations of the boss. When the boss has high expectations, that helps individuals improve their self-confidence and therefore their self-esteem. People believe that they can succeed and their performance rises to the level of their own expectations and their bosses'.
- 'Self-fulfilling prophecy' means that individuals' opinions about their ability and their own expectations about their performance largely determine their performance. People who think they can do something well will probably succeed if they have faith in themselves and are willing to work hard for it. Consequently, any actions the

boss can take that increase the employee's feelings of positive self-worth will improve the employee's performance.

How to motivate your assistant

Remember that the best person to lessen the burden of your load is your assistant. In not communicating, you make your assistant feel disrespected, forgotten, and out of the total picture. Help them to help you. Tell them what you need and want.

Show that you value your assistant by actively listening and asking appropriate questions. If you feel that your assistant is indispensable, make it known. Learn each other's strengths and weaknesses. Figure out how each other ticks. Pay attention to each other's style of thinking, learning and communicating.

Have daily (or whatever works for you both) communication meetings so that you can catch up with each other's activities. Confide in your assistant about things you are working on and let them know what your objectives are – it makes them feel involved and part of a true partnership.

Treat these meetings as you would a client meeting – stick to the time and date, make sure the door is shut so that no one pops in to see you in the middle of your communication meeting, and put the telephone through to someone else to take calls. This shows that you take the meetings seriously and you will be able to get through the tasks much more quickly. Besides, it is demotivating to be in your boss's office to have a catch-up meeting if the phone goes and you sit there waiting for the call to finish and feel that your precious time is being wasted.

Don't lay blame where it does not belong unless you have permission. (One assistant observes that: 'In the past I have allowed my boss(es) to use me as a scapegoat when they had forgotten to do something, send something, phone someone; that's okay if I know about it and agree it – in fact in some cases it was my idea.') If you have made a mistake then accept responsibility, own up to it and apologize.

Take five minutes in the morning to ask how your assistant is and be genuinely interested. That will mean you will get to know them better and be able to understand if they are not on top form that day for whatever reason, or indeed are 'hyper' because of something exciting in their home life. It's about building relationships, getting to know each other, building trust and communicating.

Encourage your assistant to join a network of like-minded colleagues and offer to pay the subscription and allow them to leave on time for monthly meetings. It is good for you and the organization for your assistant to network with counterparts from other companies, which could possibly develop business for you. These meetings are also a cost-effective way of providing training and self-development. Assistants will have the opportunity to practise, in a safe environment, skills that they may bring into the office once learnt, such as chairing meetings, giving presentations or managing events.

Ask your assistant out to lunch sometimes for a catch-up, thank-you and get-to-know-one-another exercise – it works wonders!

Conduct appraisals every six months, and talk about your goals and objectives so that your assistant can align his or her goals with you and the organization. Work on and agree some of your assistant's goals together. Give timely and constructive feedback; don't wait for the appraisals to give good or bad messages – do it at the time. If your assistant has organized an event really well, say so and congratulate him or her. Similarly, if something has not gone quite to plan, help people learn from the mistake.

Ask what motivates them and what career objectives they might have and what they are aiming to achieve.

You will be aware of how important it is in a relationship to show appreciation for the work carried out. This appreciation could be shown by a simple 'thank you' at the end of each day, taking the assistant to lunch or for a coffee and catch-up, and even nominating the assistant for an award, such as PA of the Year. When you feel appreciated it motivates you to work even harder and 'go the extra mile'.

Assistants should exceed the expectations of their boss and customers/clients by being proactive, taking on projects, continually learning and developing. The very fact that an assistant is reading this book shows self-worth and willingness to improve to become a respected and esteemed assistant.

I asked Julie Daniels, a past regular judge for *The Times* PA of the Year competition: 'What it is that the judges look for to decide who has a chance of winning a prestigious assistant award?' She replied as follows:

Candidates entering the PA of the Year award should always make sure that they supply the right information. If a CV is requested, then it's important that one is sent in. If a 500-word submission is asked for, then it's a little frustrating to receive one of 1,000 words. These are the first indicators of whether the entrant has read the instructions properly and wants to get the application right; it's also a sign of how that person will behave in a work situation.

The next thing I look for is the quality of the submission. Has the entrant written an interesting description of the job and given compelling reasons why he or she should win the award? How much value has the entrant given to his or her organization? Candidates who have been involved in projects such as building websites, marketing campaigns, company charity functions or organizing events will attract the attention of the judges more than someone who describes the more mundane aspects of an assistant's role, such as keeping a diary or taking minutes at meetings. At the final stage of the competition, the judges will speak to the shortlisted candidates to find out how well they conduct themselves at interview, and see who has the extra spark that sets them apart from the rest.

The PA of the Year award is always a difficult call. There are many outstanding applications, so it is hard to single out one particular candidate over another. At the interview, the candidate's personality comes through and so adds the final ingredient to the mix.

So now you know how you can enter the competitions and gain recognition for the job you do; make sure you build excellent working relationships and exceed your boss's, your colleagues', your customers' and even your own expectations!

Focus on the development of your assistant

Encourage your assistant to continually self-develop and learn new and challenging skills. Perhaps they could add even more value to the project work you have empowered them with. A training budget should be set aside, with a yearly allowance to pay for attendance at conferences and exhibitions, in-house training, external training, one-to-one coaching. Maybe e-learning is already set up or could be set up, and if so, time for studying in work hours should be allowed – these courses usually take no more than an hour. I have created a 'Personal strengths assessment form', shown in Appendix 1, which can be downloaded online (see front of book for details). Encourage your assistant to complete this and then devise a PDP to strengthen any weaknesses.

Read the tips below, which have come from assistants around the world. In the questionnaire I asked: 'What would you do differently or change if you were the boss for the day?' The following are some answers for bosses to mull over and think about. Alternatively, they could be ideas that assistants could take to their bosses to help them understand what the assistants want and need to improve relationships, their careers and work ethics:

- 'Don't forget to greet your assistant on arrival in the office. Take a minute or two to ask how their evening or weekend went.'

- 'If I was the boss for the day I would forbid myself to use the e-mail to communicate but pick up the phone and speak to people.'

- 'I would not give false deadlines as these often end up being the biggest time-wasters.'

- 'Bosses should praise the work that is done well and mention exactly what it was that impressed them.'

- 'Saying please now and again also helps – just being polite and having old-fashioned good manners with each other are appreciated by everyone.'

- 'I would change my diary and keep some "planning time" free to really see what's urgent and what's not, and work accordingly to move key things forward. I would also take appointments out of my diary that really don't add any value (time-wasters).'

- 'I would involve my assistant in planning the day (first, I would plan the day), and keep him/her informed about the cases we are working on.'

- 'I would have "e-mail downtime" – I would ensure that everyone turns off their e-mail for one hour in the morning and one in the afternoon.'

- 'The first thing I would do as boss for the day is initiate excellence programmes to ensure all employees are maximizing their potential and contribution (this might include job rotation, for example). The second thing would be performance measures for everyone, with a direct influence on their income.'

- 'Make the very most of my assistant at all times.'

- 'Ensure staff morale is kept at maximum by rewarding with either a good word/e-mail or a lunch out.'

- 'Ask the staff what their workload is like before insisting they do more work. Explain things in plain English, and confirm the person understands what the requirements are.'

- 'Make appointments to speak to colleagues, rather than just have an open office door. Otherwise when you are in the office people are constantly wanting to speak to you, and you are being distracted from work.'

- 'I would give my assistant access to my e-mails and encourage them to read my 'sent' e-mails to ensure transparency.'

- 'I like to get feedback from my manager, whether I have done a good job or a bad one. That way I can make changes if needed for next time.'

- 'I would swap roles for half a day to increase understanding and empathy.'

- 'I would encourage my staff to take their full annual leave allowance each year and advise that they should not feel guilty about it. This should not be the case, given that we work for a company that promotes flexible working practices and a good work–life balance.'

- 'Communicate openly. Inform employees of both successes and failures. Clearly state targets/budgets and provide facts and figures, so the employees know if they and their department are on the right track.'

- 'Provide enough staff so that excessive workloads and stress do not make employees ill.'

- 'Encourage and provide opportunities for your assistant to grow in their role. For example, invite them to participate in some of your meetings whether internal or external – possibly to take minutes, or perhaps to get their contribution. If your assistant attends management meetings with you and gets to understand the business better, how it is run and why, he or she will be able to be more proactive and will become an even more valuable asset for you.'

- 'I would eliminate any "them and us" practices that may exist, in ways ranging from ensuring that the admin team are suitably incentivized (pay/bonus) to ensuring there is adequate funding for training and development at all levels.'

- 'I would support my assistant with subscriptions for industry magazines and membership/event fees for assistant networking organizations, and would recognize how powerful these networking organizations are. I would also make sure that they could leave on time (so long as I was forewarned) to attend networking events. After all, this could benefit the boss and the organization when you consider that the assistants are seen as the "gatekeepers" to the CEOs and directors.'

The key to a successful working relationship is communication, empathy, communication, empowerment, communication, motivation and of course communication. Set your SMARTER goals of your learning programme and remember to review them continually. Keep your boss and/or organization informed of your activities even if you are organizing and paying for this yourself; this will enable them to understand your situation, particularly if you possibly need to finish on time regularly or work on projects within your organization for your qualification. Remember to make them Specific, Measurable, Agreed and aligned with your boss if appropriate, Realistic and achievable, and Time-bound because without dates set it will not happen. Remember to Evaluate your goals regularly and Revise them if appropriate.

Your relationship should be a 'partnership' that is powerful and beneficial to you both, exceeding all expectations. Your assistant can be your coach, your sounding board, your ear to the ground, your timekeeper, your buddy and your friend. Once you trust and respect each other, your assistant will be loyal, hard-working and motivated. You will both enjoy going to work more, have more fun, feel more exhilarated and satisfied that your efficient and effective working relationship will help you deliver your objectives and so help you exceed your clients' expectations, which in the end improves the bottom line.

...and on that note – a note to the boss: thank you for reading this chapter, whether it is on your own or together with your assistant. Please take action today and I wish you both a successful and mutually beneficial career.

11 Confident minute-taking

Confident minute-taking is a key skill that is appreciated by employers. It's about being prepared, practised and productive on a timely basis and having the confidence in your skills to enjoy it.

This chapter will define what minute-taking is and help you to understand the benefits of volunteering to take minutes. It will explain what preparation is required before the meeting, actions to be taken during the meeting, including understanding the different types of minutes, the importance of the relationship between the chairperson and the minute-taker and their roles, and what is required after the meeting.

Definition

Minutes are official clear, concise notes taken during a meeting to remind everyone what was discussed. They are factual and objective, void of emotions and personal thoughts, and are instrumental in taking matters forward as the actions are agreed, allocated, recorded and timed. They make a meeting worthwhile and, once agreed, cannot be disputed.

Well-written accurate minutes are an effective way of communicating, making decisions and getting things done, and are a source of information for people who were not at the meeting. They demonstrate the way an organization is accountable to its clients, its employees and any other stakeholders.

The role of the minute-taker is to prepare for the meeting in its entirety. It's a lot more than entering a meeting, sitting down to take the minutes and leaving to write them up. It's about organizing the whole experience, exceeding expectations, saving the time and energy of the chairperson (who may be your boss) and about thinking of every eventuality in order to do the best job using the appropriate skills.

Personal benefits of taking the minutes

You will:

- get to know and understand the business better and know things others do not, or at least be the first to know;
- raise your profile;
- learn excellent listening, summarizing and interpreting skills – the more you practise the better you will be;
- be perceived as part of the 'senior' team and even more so if you take part in the discussions;
- open up opportunities and career avenues and possibly be enabled to travel with the company to different offices/countries;
- understand the characters and personalities of the attendees and those who are important and the ones who make the decisions;
- be able to use these skills anywhere and add them to your CV.

Preparation

See Appendix 11 (online) which is a generic checklist for organizing meetings and events.

Pre-meeting with the chairperson

Remember that you are vital to the meeting with a very important role to play. Have confidence in yourself to set up a pre-meeting with the chairperson so that you both know what you require of each other. For subsequent similar meetings it is not necessary to have a pre-meeting every time, as you will have an understanding between you of how you should work together and what is required of each of you.

It should be agreed with the chairperson that they will summarize agenda points during the meeting to help make sure that you have understood and recorded them properly. It would be helpful to set up a signal with the chairperson in case you need clarification on any point and you wish them to either repeat someone's name for an action or clarify a point for you. You can also agree with the chairperson if it is okay for you to speak up yourself as the aim is to record accurate and meaningful notes.

"A chairperson is not always conscious of the value of summarizing, identifying speakers, clarifying decisions reached and pausing if the minute-taker leaves the room."

(Wendy Reed, Reed Learning)

Depending on what the meeting is and what the agenda topics are, it may be an opportunity for you to request to be involved with the discussion of one of the agenda items at the meeting, for example any administration items on the agenda. It is difficult to take minutes and be involved in the meeting at the same time, so offer to do this when you feel confident. The way to do it is to be prepared before you go into the meeting and know what you are going to say. If you say something in the meeting that you had not already planned, write down a few key words and then, as soon as the meeting is over, write the notes more fully or start making them into the draft minutes immediately.

Discuss with the chairperson the most appropriate place for you to sit during the meeting. The preferable place is close to the chairperson so that you can easily catch their eye or connect with them in some way and be able to hear everything that is being said. If you cannot sit close to the chairperson, sit so that you can easily hear everyone speak and where you can catch the eye of the chairperson.

Attendees

Consult with the chairperson regarding the attendee list to make sure you know who should be invited and consider whether they really need to be there for all of the meeting or just part of it. Once the attendees have been agreed, prepare an attendee list, making sure you have the correct spelling of their names. If the attendees are new to you, try to source pictures of them so that you can put names to faces. This will help you when you are taking the notes in the meeting when reporting who has said what. You may find these on your intranet if they are internal people, and the internet is very useful for finding external people.

Check with the chairperson if a 'sign-in' sheet will be required at the meeting so that you will be able to mentally put a name to a face when you see them sign in. It will be helpful during the meeting to draw a sketch of where everyone is sitting, with their names, to remind you when taking notes. Even though it may not be necessary to report on who said what in the final minutes, it is sometimes important to note it in the draft as this may be information for reference at a later date. I recommend you keep a copy of all draft minutes as well as final minutes, or at least until the next meeting when the draft minutes are accepted by everyone.

You can request that the chairperson asks the attendees to introduce themselves, which will help you identify them for minute-taking. This will depend on the type of meeting and whether people already know each other. You can suggest typing up name cards for the attendees if appropriate.

As you will be sending the invitation out, you often receive the replies of acceptance or decline, so it is your job to keep the chairperson up to date with this information. In formal meetings where voting takes place, it may be necessary to ensure that a 'quorum' is present when voting is required and it may be your job to alert the chairperson if there is not. A quorum is the number of eligible voting members of the committee that need to be present at a meeting in order for decisions to be made. For example, there may be 12 voting members and the statutes may dictate that one-third of the voting committee members need to be present, in this case four. If only three voting members turn up, the meeting would be termed 'inquorate' and any decisions that were needed would have to be deferred to the next meeting.

The agenda

The minute-taker should be familiar with the agenda, title and reason for the meeting and the objectives of the meeting to fully understand what he or she should be recording. Discuss the content and any concerns about the agenda and understand the objectives of the meeting. Discuss catering requirements if applicable and remember to include refreshments/lunch-break timing on the agenda.

Agree on the draft agenda, taking into consideration the time required for each item rather than habitually or arbitrarily deciding the length of the meeting. Keep the timings realistic – usually things take longer than you think.

Suggest that 'Matters arising' (confirmation that action points from the previous meeting have been completed) should be towards the end of the agenda so that the meeting is not taken up with the last meeting's items. If there is a lot to be discussed in 'Matters arising', these should be itemized and added as a topic and timed as part of the meeting.

There is no need to include 'Any other business' as the agenda is sent to all participants in advance of the meeting and updates/further agenda items can be added. There should not be any 'surprises' on the agenda on the day as it is better to be prepared for agenda items. Items can be brought forward to be included on the agenda for the following meeting. However, you can use 'Any other business' if you have had to call an urgent meeting at short notice and the draft agenda has not been distributed to attendees.

After liaison with the chairperson, send the draft agenda to the participants in sufficient time, asking for their input/comments. Following any comments, the agenda should be changed. You should agree the final agenda with the chairperson and then send it out again before the meeting. Once you are familiar with the work, you may be able to draft and send out the draft agenda yourself and just have a final review with the chairperson.

The style of the agenda can vary, so look at the previous agenda or in your 'Standard operating procedures' manual. Maybe you have a template for an agenda or, if you don't have a template, it may be a good idea to create one for future use.

There are two different types of agenda:

- Basic informal agenda – a list of numbered headings where everyone in the meeting understands what the headings mean, plus timings for each topic. See Appendix 7 (online) for an example of an informal agenda.

- Formal full agenda – an agenda with a lot of detail, including who is responsible for an item, the purpose, desired outcome, participation and timing. See Appendix 8 (online) for an example of a full agenda.

Supporting documentation

Make sure the attendees are aware that the agenda and supporting documentation (including the minutes from the last meeting) will be collated by the minute-taker and either copied for each attendee or e-mailed to the attendees for them to print out and bring to the meeting with them.

If there are any presentations to be given, check with the speaker if you can have a copy of the handouts to prevent having to write notes; you may wish to ask permission to attach the slides to the agenda and/or minutes.

It is also worth skim-reading the supporting documentation, which will help familiarize you with any technical jargon, spellings, abbreviations, and topics to be discussed. It will keep you one step ahead and make it less likely that you will have to clarify things during the meeting, and give you the best chance of recording correct information.

Using technology for supporting documentation

Consider using technology such as 'Diligent Boardbooks' for boardroom papers on board portals. Using a board portal is an easy, secure way to compile, manage, distribute, view and archive board meeting documents. The attendees can take their laptop, iPad/tablet etc into the meeting and be able to view the documentation, which is kept in the (computing) 'cloud' and can be seen anywhere at any time. It is also possible to project the documentation on to a big screen during the meeting. This saves paper and therefore reduces the company's carbon footprint as well as ensuring that the reams of documentation do not need to be copied, carried or filed as they are filed automatically in the 'cloud'.

Another advantage is that the papers are always up to date and easily accessible, and can even be changed in the meeting itself, thereby reducing the risk of having outdated documentation. It also eliminates a lot of photo-copying time and is excellent for those who cannot physically get to the meeting.

Technology is being developed all the time and it can make your life easier and more time efficient, so keep yourself up to date and share knowledge with peers.

You can save hours during the course of a year by using resources that are already available – eg use the templates in Microsoft Office, or my template in Appendix 9 (online). Appendix 10 (online) shows an example set of minutes using Appendix 9. You can also create your own template to suit your organization. Once created, make sure you share this with your colleagues.

During the meeting

Taking the minutes

The role of the chairperson in the meeting

The key to a successful meeting is starting and finishing on time and keeping to the timed agenda. 'Timekeeper' and 'parker' volunteers will help with this role. The 'timekeeper' makes sure that the allotted time given to each item is adhered to and the 'parker' notes down any points that need to continue to be discussed under 'Parked items' at the end of the agenda.

The agenda items should be followed. The chairperson should keep everyone aware of it and prevent the attendees from talking too long or 'waffling' on any particular item. The chairperson should also disallow any additional issues brought to the table. These items can be carried forward for the next meeting if appropriate. The chairperson should work to stimulate group discussion by asking open-ended questions and redirect questions to other members of the group to ensure that everyone contributes. He or she should watch the attendees' body language – look for signs of tiredness, exasperation and confusion, and take necessary action. The chairperson needs to manage the relationships and personalities of attendees, remind everyone of the required outcomes and steer the meeting towards making progress.

The chairperson should make sure that everyone speaks clearly and coherently (no mumbling) and that only one person at a time is speaking, so that the minute-taker can clearly hear and understand what to minute. The chairperson should make sure it is clear who is responsible for each action.

Minute-taker's role during the meeting

You may feel a little nervous before a meeting simply because you want to do a good job, and that is okay as long as you use that nervous energy to focus on the job in hand (the adrenalin may even help you to write/type faster!). If you have practised your skill, prepared well in advance and had a pre-meeting with the chairperson to agree on how you will work together, you will do an excellent and professional job.

When the attendees enter the room greet them, introduce yourself, let them know you will be taking the minutes and shake hands if appropriate (keeping religion and culture in mind). It's good for them to know who you are so that they can be more mindful of speaking clearly, spelling things out where necessary. If you have to interrupt the meeting for clarification they will understand why.

Make a note of who arrives late or leaves early, who steps out during the meeting and when they return, so that you can help them by making sure that the chairperson knows whom to brief on what they missed.

Divide those who were not at the meeting into two categories: 'Apologies' for those who let you know that they wouldn't be there, and 'Absent' ('no-shows) for those who didn't arrive but were expected. Marking someone down as 'Absent' might well embarrass them into turning up next time or at least having the courtesy to offer their apologies.

Be assertive and be prepared to ask questions for clarity. Also, if you are asked to read back part of the minutes for the attendees' clarification, speak clearly and confidently and use a tone of voice and volume that convey confidence. If you cannot break into the meeting, write down what you think was said and who said it, and go to that person immediately after the meeting to clarify your answer.

Remember to look at the speaker when deciding on what you are going to record whenever you can, in order to determine who is speaking and because it is much easier to hear when you see them speak. Many of us lip-read more than we realize! If you catch their eye it also reminds them that you are there and may prompt them to spell awkward, unusual or industry-specific words for you, clarify abbreviations etc.

Record the date of the next meeting that the attendees have agreed to.

Methods to record the minutes

Decide on the method of recording the minutes and prepare yourself so that you are working as efficiently as you can in the meeting.

You can use shorthand/longhand/short-form speedwriting or devise your own short forms as long as you can decipher them later and can write fast enough to capture the details required. If you are taking notes in a notepad, head a different page with a corresponding item heading taken from your agenda, leaving plenty of room so that if they go back and speak about a topic you can easily slot it in. This is especially useful when 'parked' items are discussed at the end of the meeting and is much better than having arrows and asterisks everywhere.

I would recommend using a spiral-bound notepad as the pages are less likely to tear out and can be easily and quickly turned over. Make sure you number each page, eg 1 of 4, 2 of 4 etc. Have your notepad ready for minute-taking by drawing a vertical line down the left-hand side of the page so that you can insert the initials of the speaker. As mentioned in the attendees section but worth mentioning again, you might not record these in the final

TABLE 11.1 How to set up your notepad for recording minutes

Agenda Item No Initials of who said what	Draft notes of minutes	Initials of who is accountable/ date of action

minutes but they are useful to keep for reference or if you need to check with the speaker on a factual point that you need to clarify. Draw a line down the right-hand side of the page where you can insert initials for allocating action points, deadlines given to the actions, asterisks, arrows, cross-referencing indicators of any kind that will help you to produce the most accurate final minutes.

You can prepare the page as illustrated in Table 11.1.

This method will prevent you mixing up who said what and who is doing which action as they will be on opposite sides of the page. If you are not sure of the name of the speaker, ask, or write down a description of them and what they are wearing and find out their name at the first convenient moment.

Heather Baker of Bakerwrite says: 'Don't try to write your minutes in the meeting. Take notes during the meeting, write your minutes afterwards. Minute-taking is not dictation and just because something is in your notes, it may not need to be included in the final summary.'

Remember to have spare pens and pencils available, and plenty of paper. Choose the best pen or pencil for you – try them out beforehand and find the pen with ink that flows easily and helps you glide over the paper and that has the most comfortable grip for you. For example, pens with a rubber grip are useful to prevent your hand from slipping.

Using technology for recording the minutes

You can use Microsoft Office OneNote for taking minute notes, which some people find really useful, and it integrates easily with all other Office programs. You can use OneNote to do an audio recording as well as a video recording. It is easy to share files via OneNote and it can show the history of page revisions. You can also sync to a 'cloud' via Windows SkyDrive. You can easily drop screenshots, drawings, pictures etc into your notes. There are free training workshops on the internet to show you how to get the best use out of OneNote if you don't already use it.

If you are taking minutes on a laptop you should use a template and have a new page open for each topic to prevent you from having to scroll up and down a document, wasting time. You can label it up ready with all agenda items inserted and as much information as you know before the meeting. Alternatively, you can create your own template, use the last set of minutes as a template or use your company-specific template. Find what works best for you and your company.

Using a laptop in the meeting saves time in deciphering your handwritten/short-form notes after the meeting, and around 80 per cent of the work of drafting the minutes is already done. Remember to check whether you need an extension lead for your laptop.

If you want to do an audio recording of a meeting, you must have the agreement of the chairperson and attendees because of 'breach of privacy'. It is quite often preferred not to record meetings, as it could inhibit participation and things may be said that should never be recorded but simply be part of the decision-making process. Other disadvantages of recording meetings are: the recording device failing to work in any part of the meeting, running out of recording time, picking up extra noises such as clacking of cups on saucers etc, not being able to decipher when more than one person is speaking, and the almost impossible task of recognizing who is speaking. It also makes the job of minute-taking twice as long, as you sit through the meeting while it is recording and then you have to listen to the whole meeting again while deciding on what you should type up as minutes. Most importantly, if the chairperson should ask you to read back what was minuted in, for example, topic 4, you cannot do this with recording alone; you would still have to write the notes in the meeting and use the recording as a back-up. Make sure that the recording is deleted when minutes are agreed and that you have permission to do so.

You can use a digital smartpen for writing minutes, such as a Livescribe smartpen. This pen records everything you hear and write in a Livescribe notebook. It has a 2 GB memory, and if you are struggling to read a word you have written when you are trying to read it back (whether in the meeting or later), you simply tap on the word with your pen and the pen reads it out for you. Your written notes can be reviewed onscreen using the software as well as on paper, as every page of your notebook is uploaded to your computer, so your notes are safe (even if you lose your original notebook), searchable and reviewable. The software makes it simple to share your handwritten notes, images and diagrams together with recorded audio. The smartpen creates an interactive PDF document with sound, known as a pencast, from the page or notes you want to share. If you send this pencast – via e-mail, Google Docs or other connectors, the recipient can click on the notes or image and listen to the audio that goes with it. You can send pencasts to an iPhone or iPad and the recipient can click on the screen to hear your message. There are also apps such as language translators where you can write a word in English, tap on it and the smartpen translates it into a different language such as Spanish. Other useful apps include Wikipedia and a spell checker.

Another technological solution for taking minutes is using websites which are free and simple to use. For example, **www.minutes.io** has a service for recording action points in a meeting and sharing them with all meeting participants. Once you have typed in all the attendees' names you can quickly 'pick up' their name when assigning them to an action. The calendar pops up for you to put in the 'due date' and you can type in the 'note' section. The drafts are saved in your browser waiting to be sent when you are back online (if you are not online during the meeting). In addition to e-mailing the minutes on your behalf, minutes.io publishes them using secret URLs, making it easy to access them from anywhere. You will then receive a personalized e-mail with your 'to-dos' easily grouped for you.

Format of minutes

Review the previous minutes and remind yourself of the topics and what happened last time, and this will help you better understand the meeting you are about to take the minutes for. If you did not take the previous minutes then take a note of the layout and type of minutes written, including the amount of detail and the phrases used. Also look to see if any abbreviations are used and familiarize yourself with them. Check with peers (who may have taken the minutes before) if there are any industry-specific words/

scientific names/jargon that you may not understand – and familiarize yourself with them.

If this is the first meeting and there are no previous minutes, agree with the chairperson the type of meeting it is to be, for example formal or informal, the type of minutes required for the meeting and if there are any industry-specific words that you may need to know about.

The level of formality and the type of minutes required will depend on:

- tradition;
- size of your organization;
- culture of the organization;
- the type of meeting it is.

Different types of minutes

Minutes can be either 'open' minutes which can be seen by everyone and in the public domain or 'closed' minutes which will be seen only by the group of people for whom they are written. However, even closed minutes may eventually be declassified as soon as there is no organizational interest or personal privacy to protect. What is written in minutes is there forever, so be mindful of what you write.

There is no standard level of detail in minutes and people tend to do a mix of the different styles – you need to find what suits you, your boss and your organization.

Six main styles of minutes are:

1 **Board minutes**. Board minutes are formal and more traditional and you have to think what is needed to satisfy the shareholders. These have a lot more content than simply summarizing and you have to take time to read these minutes. These are used for meetings such as annual general meetings and formal board meetings. Formal minutes follow a set structure, decisions are proposed, seconded and voted upon, formal language is used and may address people formally.

   For any items to be voted upon you should copy motions, amendments and other items word for word. Record whether motions/proposals are adopted or rejected, who made the motion and who seconded, how the vote is taken (by show of hands, voice or other method), and record the numbers of votes for approval, oppose and abstain. If voting members arrive late or have to leave early, the precise point when they arrived or left the meeting should be noted.

2 **Attributed minutes.** Attributed minutes report who said what.

3 **Verbatim.** There are still some meetings that require verbatim minutes. People speak on average 125 wpm and you would therefore need shorthand or short-form speedwriting to get it down word for word, or you could record it and type it up like dictation. You can challenge your chairperson if they request verbatim and ask the questions: Who is reading it and do you really need every word? Is it really worth it?

Verbatim minutes are required, for example, in court, for human resource issues such as disciplinary proceedings, grievances and parliamentary proceedings.

4 **Mind mapping.** Mind mapping can be done either freehand or with a technical program on a laptop as the meeting takes place and connected to a projector if required. It is good for brainstorming and memory recall and can be used for team meetings.

5 **Action points.** Small internal groups such as teams or advisory or project groups are likely to produce action point minutes. The purpose of these minutes is to provide a record of decisions that require action and are focused on moving forward – they will require the following questions answered:
   - Who is accountable?
   - What is the action and by when?

6 **Summary minutes.** Summary minutes are the most popular and the most preferable as they are short and concise – it is better to have two pages to read than six pages simply filed away and not read! You should still write in sentences and you can use some bullet point lists to keep the minutes brief. The essence and the messages of the meeting should be summarized. You should listen for the decisions, action points, reasons and content of discussion and the difference between fact and opinion. The minutes are an objective account of what happened in the meeting and not a reflection of what any one person thinks should be in them. Remember to write the name or initials of the person assigned to an action point.

> *"The decisions and action points are the main things to record, everything else is a luxury. TIP: Spend less time writing and more time listening, understanding and interpreting."*
> (Wendy Reed, Reed Learning)

Think about who is on the distribution list and whether anyone receiving the minutes did not attend the meeting. If the item is complicated you may wish to note more content, such as the reasons why a decision was reached or important points that were made. If the item is controversial, you should note down key points for and against the decision.

Summary minutes are usually for informal meetings such as committee meetings and subcommittee meetings.

Practicalities

- Do not wear jewellery on your wrists that will prevent you from taking notes easily and also may be noisy on the table. Be careful about long nails which may press the wrong keys and make a distracting noise in the meeting.

- Make sure you are able to sit comfortably with your back supported, using as many of the ergonomic tips given in Chapter 8 as possible. If you cannot work at a table, make sure you have a firm clipboard to rest your notepad on, or a laptop tray.

Listening skills for minute-taking

As most people speak approximately 125 words a minute and as the mind processes words at around 400–500 words per minute, we often let our minds wander during the gap between what they are saying and how quickly we process it.

Therefore, it is important to recognize your own barriers to active listening while taking minutes so that you can overcome them in order to help you maintain concentration and capture the key information. Table 11.2 sets out barriers and solutions to listening during minute-taking.

What should be reported in the minutes?

The chairperson will clarify the type of minutes and the amount of detail required (see types of minutes above). Listen carefully for comments which should never be written in the minutes – you will normally be told that 'this is off the record' and the chairperson will affirm this.

TABLE 11.2 Barriers to listening during minute-taking and solutions

Barriers to listening	Solutions to barriers
Your nerves if worried about taking the minutes	<ul><li>Take deep breaths to introduce oxygen and calmness into your body.</li><li>Be prepared.</li><li>Practise until you feel confident.</li></ul>
Boredom – due to lack of understanding	Pre-read material so that you get to understand more about what is being discussed. The fact that you have an interest in what is being said will alleviate boredom.
Boredom – due to repetition of the same thing being discussed	Tell the chairman that it has been discussed before and ask if you need to minute it again (this may make the chairman take better control of the meeting).
You may start getting emotive and thinking of your opinion on the subject being discussed	Remain impartial and in control of your emotions – you are simply there to take the minutes, not get involved (unless your involvement has been organized beforehand).
Distractions such as noises like a projector or air conditioning	Sit as far away from the noise as possible, remembering to keep your positioning with the chairman, and focus on the speaker, shutting everything else out. You may need to ask them to speak up over the noise if nothing can be done about it.
Distractions such as looking out of the window or looking at what's going on outside the room through windows, and glass doors and walls	<ul><li>Position yourself away from windows and/or close blinds.</li><li>Keep windows and doors closed to minimize outside noise.</li></ul>
Low speaking voices/mumbling	Ask the person to speak louder/more clearly or signal to the chairperson that you need them to say something on your behalf.

TABLE 11.2 *Continued*

Barriers to listening	Solutions to barriers
Trying to remember people's names to attribute the discussion to them instead of listening to what is being said	• Ask the chairperson to get the attendees to introduce themselves at the beginning of the meeting or before they speak. • Use the table plan that you put together at the beginning of the meeting. • Send a registration sheet of paper round once attendees are seated and ask them to write their name on it (not a typed list to sign as it may not be in the right order). • Have name place cards. • Ask the attendee their name as they finish speaking.
Trying to understand technical words and thereby missing what comes next	Familiarize yourself with technical and industry-specific words before the meeting – look at the last meeting minutes, ask the chairman in the pre-meeting.
Hunger	Make sure you have eaten before you go into the meeting.
Too hot or too cold	• Before the meeting starts, ensure that you know where the temperature control is or have a phone number of someone who does and get it right before the meeting starts. • If it becomes too hot or cold during the meeting, tell the chairperson as the attendees will probably feel uncomfortable too. • If you have to leave the room to sort anything out during the meeting, either ask the chairperson for a break or ask someone to take the notes while you are out of the room.

You don't need to worry too much about writing more than you need in the meeting. Remember that what you write/type in the meeting is simply your notes. Therefore, when you type up your draft minutes for the chairperson's review after the meeting, you can leave out what you deem to be irrelevant, making the minutes as concise and clear as possible, and written in the format requested by the chairperson. Remember to keep your notes on file to refer back to, including attributing discussion points to people. If the chairperson or an attendee decides they would like a little more detail, you can retrieve it from your notes, and remember: you can always attach presentations as supporting documentation to help keep the minutes concise. The more experience you acquire in taking minutes, the better you will understand how your chairperson and organization would like them written, and eventually it will become easier during the meeting to write exactly what is required and nothing else.

The key to writing your notes is to listen for the facts with the intent of summarizing the message and essence of the item before writing it down. Do not be influenced by the speaker's intonation, reference or emotions – focus on filtering out the discussion and avoid writing down too much detail for the type of minutes you have been requested to produce. Ask yourself the following questions:

- Is this important information and do I need to capture this?
- Is this an action item and to whom do I attribute it?
- What is the deadline given to the action?

If flip charts have been used during the meeting, make sure that you collect the used flip-chart paper before you leave the room so that you can include its content in your notes if appropriate. Also, if a 'whiteboard' has been used, you can either copy the information down or have a camera phone with you (on silent) and take a picture.

Below is an example of a set of minutes which can also be found in Appendix 10 online (see front of book for details).

Minutes of XXXX meeting

Date/time:	Friday 18 August [year], 10.00 am – 12 noon
Location:	The Boardroom, The Office
Chairperson:	Rob Waring
Minute-taker:	Sue Frantz
Timekeeper:	Samantha Hughes
Parker:	Carol Muller
Present:	Rob Waring (RW), Laura House (LH), Anne Jackson (AJ), Michael Spear (MS), Barbara Stillman (BS), Carol Muller (CM), Sue Frantz (SF), Samantha Hughes (SH)
Apologies:	Angela Smith
Absent:	Anthony Brown
Attachments:	UK Business Form Highlight of European Business Forms

Record of action points only:

Item	Action	By when?	Responsible for action
4	Think of a different icebreaker for next meeting to continue team building	17/12/ year	RW
5	Each member agreed to approach at least one company with a presence in 50% of the European countries to try to secure a partnership deal.	31/8/ year	All
5.1	RW to speak to Angela Smith and Anthony Brown to inform them of their action points.	15/12/ year	RW

Item	Action	By when?	Responsible for action
5.2	All responsible to organize regional events every 4 weeks	15/12/ year	All
6.1	Interview the EUMA PA of the Year on top tips for the newsletter	30/8/ year	AJ
6.2	Newsletter – sell advertising space to office stationery companies	30/9/ year	BS/LH

Record of meeting:

Item	Topic and description	Responsibility
1/2/ 3	Appointments/Apologies/Absent Appointment of Minute-taker, Timekeeper and Parker as indicated above	RW
4	Welcome/icebreaker The icebreaker was successful, attendees introduced themselves and team building was achieved	RW
5	Feedback from Luxembourg meeting:	RW
5.1	European Partner: The group were informed that the aim of the Committee is to gain more European partners to expand membership, obtain sponsorship and for mutual benefit of both	
5.2	Business Update: Highlights of the Business Update Forms were read out to the members (copy attached). It was noted that Europe were very pleased with the UK's submission (copy attached)	

Item	Topic and description	Responsibility
6	Newsletter	MS
6.1	Articles It was discussed that articles are required for the monthly newsletter for interest and learning	
6.2	Advertising In order to raise money for the organization we need to sell advertising. It was decided to try to sell advertising space to PA-related suppliers	
6	'Parked' item – no items were parked	
7	Date of next meeting: To be held on 18 December [year]	

Chairperson's signature ...Rob Waring......
Typist's initials / Date SF 21 August [year]

After the meeting

Producing the draft minutes from your notes

You should block out time in your diary to write up the draft minutes as quickly as possible after the meeting while the information is still fresh in your mind and to get it off your to-do list. Remember that the minutes should be written in the same order as the agenda. If you have typed the notes in the meeting, you still need to make these notes into draft minutes ready for the chairperson's review and approval. Below are some important writing tips:

- The minutes should be written in the past tense as they report on what happened in the meeting (which happened in the past) and because they are being signed and accepted at the next meeting. However, actions should be written in the future tense as they are still to be actioned.

- Active language should be used. This is more specific, clearer and shorter than passive language and therefore less likely to result in confusion. An example of active language in attributed minutes is 'Sue reported on...'. And an example of passive is 'A report was given by Sue on...'.

- The minutes should be written in the third person, so you do not make reference to I, you, we, our or your.

- In the attendees list you should include full names. You can put their initials after the names in brackets, which enables you to refer to initials throughout the minutes (if they are attributed minutes).

- The name of the minute-taker should be indicated, either under the heading 'In attendance' or next to the heading 'Minute-taker', as opposed to being included in the attendee list.

- Remember to proofread your minutes thoroughly (more on this below).

Use clear writing techniques – 'ABC':

Accuracy – make sure there are no mistakes, spelling errors or ambiguous words.

Brevity – use simple words and phrases. Sentences should be no longer than 20 words and they should be to the point. Avoid clichés like 'in this day and age'.

Clarity – use active language where possible, say things only once, make use of paragraphs and don't give people the chance to make incorrect assumptions.

Tips on proofreading

In order to proofread your work you should read forwards for sense and grammar and read bottom up and backwards for spelling. The computer spell checker should not be trusted as it will not highlight words which are spelt correctly but mean something different. Also, depending on whether you write British English or American English, the spelling errors may not be picked up for the culture you are working in. It is always a good idea to let someone else proofread your work, as a fresh pair of eyes can see things you will probably keep missing – possibly the chairperson might take this role.

Double-space your draft minutes so that handwritten corrections can easily be inserted into the document by the chairperson during their review.

The chairperson may have a different opinion on how to write minutes – even though you have produced excellent minutes. It may simply be a preference, so keep positive if they are changed and remember their style for the next time you have to write them.

"Don't get disheartened by corrections or take things personally."
(Wendy Reed, Reed Learning)

Producing the final minutes

When your minutes are being made final, make sure that the pages are numbered and the layout attractive, using your company's standard if appropriate. Never separate a heading from the body of the paragraph at a page end – always move the heading to the next page.

If anyone calls you to let you know that there are changes to be made, you cannot make the changes until they have been discussed and accepted at the next meeting. Remember always to make your notes legible and to take them with you to the next meeting in case of any disputes. Your notes are the legal record until the minutes have been formally agreed.

Distribution of minutes

Once approved and signed off by the chairperson, a final set of minutes plus attachments can be sent to all attendees, plus the people who should have attended the meeting but gave apologies and anyone else requiring the minutes, especially if they are involved with the action points. It is not best practice to assign action points to people who are not in the meeting, though sometimes it is necessary (of course, they should be informed before they receive the minutes).

Check with the chairperson how they would prefer the minutes to be distributed. The minutes could be distributed as hard copies, by e-mail, in a shared document on the hard drive, on a meetings portal on the intranet, or via your preferred social media service, which would also give you a printer-friendly option to print out the documents on file-sharing sites such as Dropbox, Google Docs, Slideshare, Microsoft SkyDrive and many others that include private settings.

File minutes chronologically together with the draft notes which will contain more detail for back-up and referral.

Follow-up

It is the minute-taker's role to follow up the action points listed in the minutes to make sure that these are completed ready for the next meeting or by when the deadline was fixed. Every action must be a clear statement of the next step with a responsible person and a deadline; the minutes of the meeting on/after that deadline should show that it was completed, abandoned or is ongoing, showing how much has been done and with the next stage shown as an action with a new deadline. The 'Matters arising' item will be on the next agenda as a status follow-up to the actions.

> "'Matters arising' is an audit trail: it shows exactly what happened about an action. Always write actions and the subsequent matters arising(s) so that a complete outsider could understand and follow them through until finished."
>
> (Joanna Gutmann, author of *Taking Minutes of Meetings*)

Remember that minute-taking can raise your profile by increasing your visibility to the management team and the attendees of the meeting. You will learn and understand more about the people and the company you work for and be privileged to hear confidential information which in turn will help you make informed decisions and be able to perform your everyday role to the best of your ability.

Now it's up to you!

To help increase your confidence, practise minute-taking by watching and listening to television programmes such as the news, interviews or chat shows. The internet and YouTube are also great sources for practising minute-taking and you will learn a lot too. The more you practise the more confident you will feel, and you may even learn to enjoy your new skill!

Minute-taking skills are invaluable to companies and can open up a whole new realm of work for you. Grasp opportunities as they arise, make opportunities for yourself and be confident and proud of the work you do.

Harnessing the power of social media

In this chapter you will learn how to harness the power of social media, concentrating mainly on the steps needed to get involved with three popular social media websites – LinkedIn, Facebook and Twitter. The chapter also mentions several other useful sites and tools to help you in your job. Throughout the chapter you will find examples and case studies of how bosses and assistants use social media.

Social media are a dynamic and rapidly developing area. While this chapter gives you an understanding of how useful social media are, I encourage you to explore them and increase your skill set to secure your future.

Warren Cass, social media marketing expert, states: 'Social media are complex because they are about personality, being authentic, being engaging and if you get them wrong they can be very unforgiving'. So follow the guidelines in this chapter and get it right from the start.

The first step to using social media is to sign up

All sites have help features, explanations, tutorials, troubleshooting tips of how best to use their sites – explore all their features and use them to your advantage.

Each site is about connecting with other people; it is easy to set up connections and just as easy to remove them.

Username

The first stage when signing up to Facebook, Twitter, LinkedIn or indeed any other social media site is to make your username as close to your real name as possible, to make it easier for people to recognize you. It helps you look like a real, authentic professional person. If you are representing a company, the name and picture/logo should reflect the company name, or you could have a combination of your name and your company name.

The second step is to create a professional, credible profile. Your profile acts like your CV, your advert, your business card and the first impression people have about you. It is best practice to keep your profile current and each social media site provides clear and concise instructions on how to set it up. Be as descriptive as possible, using keywords so that you can be found easily. You have the opportunity to write a lot more than in your CV or your 'elevator pitch', so use it and bring your passion to life, explain what you have to offer, direct people to your website, videos, recommendations, blogs or anything that can promote you. This is a fantastic opportunity to convince people to connect with you and even for recruiters to think about offering you a job (whether you are looking for one or not!). Complete your headline, summary and specialities section and make your wording keyword rich. You can move your LinkedIn profile sections into a different order if you feel that adds more value.

> Make the right first impression. It is important to choose a professional, head and shoulder, 'smiley' photo – not one of your fluffy cat (no matter how cute) or a cartoon – one that says something about you as a professional person. People want to see the real you, otherwise your credibility will be questioned.

Appendix 6 shows a list of positive adjectives to use in your profile, personal branding and/or company branding as well as your CV/résumé to describe you/your company. The appendix also includes separately a list of action verbs that you can use regarding your achievements. You can download Appendix 6 online.

Your professional profile will influence how you are perceived and it will be your personal branding. Remember to be truthful and genuine so that your profile reflects your personality. When you're happy with your profile you can add a link from Facebook, Twitter and LinkedIn to your website and/or e-mail signature to help make more connections.

Social media privacy settings

Privacy settings make your social networking more secure and manageable. You can determine exactly who can see what from your profile, posts and photos, giving you control over what you share.

The third stage is to get people to connect with you/follow you. Each social media channel has a dedicated search to help you find some useful connections. A great way of increasing your connections is to take a look at who your connections are connected to. You can also encourage people to ask you to connect with them by using the tools available to create 'Follow' buttons on your blog, website and in your signature. Similarly, your social media contact details should also be added to your business cards.

The fourth stage is to keep on communicating and building relationships. Make sure you write interesting updates that reflect your personality to attract people to want to connect with you.

Suggestions for useful updates/tweets:

- Post a link on interesting news, articles or YouTube video.

- Let followers or connections know of any offers, newsletters and e-books, some of which may be free.

- Reply to requests for help and advice whenever you feel you are knowledgeable enough to do so.

- Share a link to the next real-time or virtual conference you plan to attend (anyone around the world can attend the virtual conference).

- Post a link to your most recent company or personal blog article.

- Share pictures that can help promote you (eg of your recent business trip, but remember to choose your pictures carefully!).

- Forward on other people's updates/tweets. On Twitter you can 'Retweet' (using 'RT' or 'Retweet' at the beginning of the message or clicking Twitter's Retweet button).

- Show customers a behind-the-scenes view to showcase your expertise, integrity and knowledge.

- Write updates specifically designed to build rapport, encourage customer retention and create interest (eg 'That was a great EUMA conference – here are some photos from the gala dinner').

- Celebrating success – other people's ('Well done to the PA of the Year...') and your own ('I got the job and start on Monday!').

- Celebrating a client's/delegate's/supplier's/customer's success – show just how successful your delegates become when they follow your advice or use your products and services ('Congratulations to the senior executive assistant who acted on my advice in my workshop and is now the office manager!').

- Boost the profile of your business partners so that they get recognized for doing a good job ('Congratulations to The Office for a superb PA conference and exhibition – EUMA gained 20 new members and 180 new prospective members').

- Charity – show your commitment to corporate social responsibility or your personal commitment to charity.

- Competitions – reward your contacts/customers/clients for 'liking' your page and let them know they can win something (eg 'Looking for the PA of the Year – Click on the link to find out more...').

- Discounts – award your contacts a discount just for being connected (eg 'If you connect with me, I will give you 20% off the price of my book').

- Compliment your connections and thank them – actively build strong, trusting and respectful relationships by interacting with your connections, even if it is simply to thank them for a 'retweet' of something you posted. In return, retweet their messages to your contacts.

Social media time management

Use your discretion and common sense on how often you should use social media. Even if it is part of your role, 15 minutes in the morning and afternoon should suffice. You should never do it in work time if it is for personal use – this is neither professional nor productive for your daily workload.

To save time, you can automate scheduled updates, monitor all channels and analyse traffic using tools such as Tweetdeck, HootSuite and SocialOomph. You can connect your social media channels so that your information is put in once and is sent to all the channels you choose at the same time. Automation can be useful when connecting with countries with different time zones; when you are on holiday; unavailable for a few days; or if you are taking part in a launch event. However, used too much this could be perceived as being lazy and it can appear that you are connecting just for the sake of it; so use it wisely. Keep in mind that no one wants to build relationships with an automated robot. You should respond in a timely and polite way to keep your connections interested and accept connection requests on a timely basis.

Warning!

When on social media you are in the public domain, what you put out there stays out there and can get passed around. People have lost their jobs through inappropriate use of social media and writing things that entitle their company to dismiss them legally and immediately. Others have been dismissed from work for saying inappropriate things about their colleagues and bosses. You should realize that all recruiters, prospective employers and headhunters actively use social media to find out about prospective employees, forthcoming interviewees and their current employees.

Cyber bullying and its consequences are the same as face-to-face bullying and if you experience this you should report it immediately to your employer and/or the police.

Below you will find the main features and glossaries for Twitter, Facebook and LinkedIn; these are not exhaustive but you will be able to get started and understand how and why you should use them. Once you understand and use the basics, look at each site individually and see what else you can make use of.

Twitter

People's first reaction to Twitter is often: 'No one needs to know what I'm doing' and 'I don't care what other people are doing.' This section will help to clarify the value that Twitter can provide as it is a useful communication tool that allows you to interact with people around the world in three different ways:

1 Send a short message to a group of people publicly.

2 Send a short message to a specific person publicly.

3 Send a short message to a specific person privately.

Twitter is best used for timely updates, information sharing and relationship building, especially useful for public relations and promotions.

To get a Twitter account: go to **http://twitter.com**, click the sign up button and select your username and password. To connect to people on Twitter you do not need their permission and you do it by 'following' them by clicking the 'follow' button on their profile. They will know you are following them and will most likely follow you back. When you 'follow' someone, every time they post a new tweet, it will appear on your Twitter home page and you can also have them coming through to your mobile phone.

Twitter has a 'Who to follow button' which suggests people to follow who are similar to the ones you already follow.

Twitter gives you the option to create a customized background – either use a design that Twitter offers and change the colours or upload a logo or appropriate picture to make it unique. You will find it in 'settings', 'design'.

Twitter vocabulary explained

Twitter username is the name you select to represent yourself on Twitter and it always starts with the @ sign. Mine is @suefrance – follow me!

To Follow: To subscribe to someone's updates on Twitter, click the 'Follow' button on that person's Twitter page, which can be found for me at **http://twitter.com/@suefrance**. When you follow someone, their updates will be displayed on your Twitter homepage.

To Follow Back: To do this you need to subscribe to the updates of someone who has recently started following you. In Twitter's notifications settings, you can indicate whether you'd like to receive an e-mail alert whenever a new person follows you. In the e-mail, there will be a link to that person's profile. By clicking the link, you can check out who they are and decide to follow them back or not.

> Don't follow too many people at once: best practice is to follow no more than 25 people a day, because there will be a time gap between following people and when they follow you back (not everyone will). If your profile says you are following 1,000 people and only 20 people have followed you back so far, it appears that 980 of the people you followed chose not to follow you back, which could influence people's decisions to follow you.

Tweet (or update): Each update can be no longer than 140 characters. You can post a tweet in the white text box under 'What's Happening'.

Putting @USERNAME in the very beginning of your tweet makes your tweet viewable only in the Twitter streams of people who follow you and the user to whom you're tweeting. For example: to send a tweet to be viewable by everyone and the person I intend it to go to, I could write 'Looking forward to seeing you at my PA Master Class @username on 17 November' – this advertises my Master class to everyone plus the person I am intending it to go to (in this case @ username). If I put @username looking forward to seeing you at my Master class it would only be viewed by @username and me.

@Reply: is a public message sent from one Twitter user to another. By putting @USERNAME within your tweet, Twitter knows who to send it to. This type of tweet is also called a reply or @reply. All of the @replies you receive will go into your @Mentions tab.

Direct Message (or DM): A private message sent from one Twitter user to another, by either clicking the message link on their profile or typing D USERNAME. You can set up your notifications to receive an e-mail with the direct message, and it will also go into the message tab.

Twitter Stream: A list of a person's real-time updates. Every time you post an update, it goes into your Twitter stream, which is found on your account page.

Tweet-Up: An event specifically organized for Twitter users to meet up and network, usually informally on a face-to-face basis.

Hashtag (#): The # is used to mark keywords or topics in a tweet and it was created to categorize messages. If you are looking for tweets on anything to do with recipes, put #recipe in the search box and all the tweets that have the word 'recipe' in them will be brought up. Hashtags can occur anywhere in the tweet. They can easily be created by combining a # with a word, acronym or phrase (#WORD) and used as a tag within tweets. You can use # to promote events, and people often use # when tweeting live events (ie tweeting what they see/hear in real time). The hashtag will tag and aggregate the event's tweets, building an online conversation around it. People who are not at the event might see your # and want to follow and/or join the conversation, too. A popular # often sparks curiosity, and people will go to **http://search.twitter.com** to participate in the conversation around an event.

Retweet (or RT): To repeat what someone else has already tweeted. People do this if someone has said something especially valuable and they want their own network to see the information too.

Twitter Lists: Twitter Lists generate Twitter streams that include specific users. For example, I have created a list of executive assistants in order to see their tweets and understand what their concerns are so that I can tailor my training.

Lists act as filters and snapshots of activity for certain projects, areas of interest, journalists or competitors. Lists can be set as private or public.

> *"I use Twitter lists to follow peers, airlines, weather, and traffic issues as access to an instant, almost real-time resource. It is tremendously beneficial to set up a list that is directly relevant to your employer's industry in order to have a better, big-picture perspective of the workplace."*
>
> (Kemetia MK Foley – IAAP Chapter Leader – Washington, DC, United States)

Trending Topics: Displayed on the right-hand side of your Twitter homepage, trending topics are words, phrases, or hashtags that are popular (trending) on Twitter at a given time.

Twitter Chats: Twitter has helped form an abundance of micro-communities that have self-organized around certain topics. Chats are organized discussions that happen on a set day and at a time, eg #adminchat led by an expert to discuss current issues, problems, trends etc for assistants. You can track the conversations using hashtags (#) followed by the name of the chat. You can source chats through using Google or create your own.

Facebook

Facebook is both a social-focused platform and business focused, with company pages becoming more popular. It is useful for consumer products and business events (awards ceremonies, charity fun days etc) and you can easily upload your photos. To get a Facebook account, go to **http://facebook.com** and sign up.

Friends – is the terminology given to everyone you connect with, even if it is on your company page. To add 'friends', search for a profile/timeline using the search bar at the top of any Facebook page. Click on the 'Add as Friend' button to the right of their name and a 'friend' request will be sent to that person. Once they confirm, they will show up on your list of Facebook 'friends'.

Facebook can be used in business for networking, locating business leads, as a method of intercompany communication and as a platform to organize and track events.

You can write updates and leave messages; your 'friends' can leave you messages, browse through your photo collections, or even chat with you while you are online.

Should you be 'friends' with your boss on Facebook? I know some of you have been asked to be a 'friend' of your boss on social media – my advice is to remember that everything, including pictures, that is put on social media about you, by you and by others (whom you have little control over) can be seen by everyone. Things can be misinterpreted and taken the wrong way and I would advise you to gently decline the boss's request just to be on the safe side. If you find this too difficult to do, you could put them on your 'restricted list' so that they can only see certain things.

Messenger is a separate app, so it only takes one click to get to your messages or send a new one. Messages are delivered through notifications and texts, so your friends are more likely to get them right away.

You can use Messenger to reach all of your friends – whether they're on Facebook or in your phone contacts. All you have to do is type the person's name.

However, below is a case study where sharing Facebook with your boss can work well, and your final decision on whether to add them or not will depend on your role and your relationship with your boss.

> "My relationship with my two execs, management team and colleagues is one where I am happy to be friends with them on Facebook. We use it to communicate outside work hours and share information as you would with a friend outside work. We also communicate using text messaging and iPhone apps like 'Words with Friends' and 'iMessage'. I find Facebook to be a fantastic tool to stay in touch with colleagues who are working outside the office in remote or project offices. We are a tight-knit team and it provides a level of caring and interest that I find extremely valuable."
>
> (Beth Ruge, Australia)

Be my 'friend' on my company page at **www.facebook.com/suefrancetraining**.

Profile (timeline) – your timeline/profile can make a visual history of everything you've ever done, even from when you were born! Facebook automatically adds photos, status updates and life events from your Facebook history to your timeline, though you can also choose photos and content. You can decide which groups you want to share this with: Public, Friends, Friends of Friends, or specific people in the custom field. You can decide exactly who can see your e-mail address, where you work, and who is in your family. You can control which posts, photos and tags appear on your profile. Profiles (timelines) are meant for individual people; they are not suited to meeting business needs.

Like – 'Like' is a way to give positive feedback. Liking a 'Page' means you are connecting to that Page. When you connect to a Page, it will appear in your profile (timeline) and you will appear on the Page as a person who likes that Page. The Page will also be able to post content into your News Feed. You always have control over your connections. You can 'unlike' something or control who can see your likes on your profile (timeline).

Pages – Pages allow organizations, businesses, celebrities and brands to communicate broadly with people who 'like' them. Pages may be created and managed only by official representatives. Page information and posts are public and generally available to everyone on Facebook. Anyone can like a Page to become connected with it and get News Feed updates. Page admins can share posts under the Page's name. Page posts appear in the News Feed of people who like the Page. Page admins can also create customized tabs for their Pages and check Page Insights to track growth and activity.

Groups – Groups provide a closed space for small groups of people to communicate about shared interests and can be created by anyone. In addition to an open setting, more privacy settings are available for groups. In closed groups, posts are only visible to group members. Group members must be approved or added by other members. Members receive notifications by default when any member posts in the group and can participate in chats, upload photos to shared albums, collaborate on group docs, and invite all members to group events.

Wall – The 'Wall' is where you write comments on what you are up to, or share photos and articles. You'll also see what your 'friends' are posting on their Wall, and anyone on your friend's list can write a comment on your Wall.

Online photo album – Facebook is a great place to upload photos but remember to keep them professional at all times! Uploading them to Facebook means that anyone can look anytime and share photos by 'tagging' people in. For example, whenever I hold workshops I take photos with the permission of the delegates and put them on my Facebook company page.

Tag – A tag links a person, page, or place to something you post, like a status update or a photo. For example, you can tag a photo to say who is in the photo or post a status update and say who you are with.

When you 'tag' someone, they will be notified. Also, if you tag someone in your post and it's sent to a friend, the post is visible to the audience you selected plus friends of the tagged person. The tagged post also goes on your profile (timeline).

Block – You can block anyone from seeing your profile, adding you as a friend and sending your messages and become invisible to each other on Facebook.

Events – You can create two types of events: a public event, available for anyone to RSVP and attend, and a private event. Private events will only be visible to people who have been invited, and only invited people can see the event in their News Feed. The people you invite will be able to post messages, photos, videos and links on the event's Wall.

Facebook Messenger – When your 'friends' are on Facebook at the same time as you, you can direct message them and have a private conversation with them in real time.

Lists – Lists are optional and you can easily add friends to the right lists. Types of lists are:

Smart lists – These lists create themselves and stay up to date based on profile information your friends have in common with you, like your work, school, family and city:

Close Friends list – Add your friends and family to your Close Friends list and you'll see everything they post in News Feed. You can receive notifications when they post updates, so you don't miss anything important.

Acquaintances list – Add business contacts to your Acquaintances list and you'll only see what Facebook consider to be the important things they post so you keep in touch. You can choose to exclude these people when you are posting something.

Restricted list – Is for people you have added as a friend and they will only be able to see the content that you make public or that you tag them in. Whoever you add to this list will not be notified or aware of it.

LinkedIn

LinkedIn is a leading business social network, a useful recruitment tool, good for information sharing with groups of interest, and with powerful search facilities. To get a LinkedIn account, go to **http://LinkedIn.com** and sign up.

To add connections on LinkedIn, simply search for people you know, such as old friends and colleagues, industry professionals, recruiters, trainers, and you can join LinkedIn groups with like-minded people. When you take part in discussions or start discussions, other people will start to notice you and you can request a connection, and they may ask you to connect too. Add 'friends' to Facebook by clicking 'Like' on any Facebook Page, using the 'find friends' feature and accepting requests.

Tools like 'Answers' and 'Groups' let you locate and interact with experts. Whether you're looking for a career opportunity, winning new clients or building your professional reputation, LinkedIn connects you to jobs, sales leads and ideal business partners.

LinkedIn connects you to your trusted contacts and helps you exchange knowledge, ideas and opportunities with a broader network of professionals. It is much more than a recruitment tool, with discussion groups of interest and powerful search facilities.

In today's professional world, people change jobs and locations regularly. By connecting on LinkedIn, your address book will never go out of date. Your contacts update their profiles, keeping you current with their latest jobs, projects and contact information.

Discussion groups

There are many different types of groups on LinkedIn and you are allowed to belong to 50 of them at any one time. You can create your own groups and I have created one called 'Tips for Office Professionals Worldwide with Sue France Training' – join me and connect with me at **www.linkedin.com/suefrance**.

There are many discussion groups to choose from on LinkedIn that are relevant to your field; you can receive a lot of great advice, tips and tricks of the trade. Consider LinkedIn as a 'career resource'. You're never too old to learn new things.

Jasmine Freeman, assistant to Joan Burge, points out that when you provide a relevant comment on a forum you are actually rated. It's worth bearing this in mind as if you receive positive ratings, people may want to seek you out, which could lead to opportunities in the future.

Advanced Search tool – Find exactly what you're looking for, whether it is to make new connections, specific skill sets or find subject-matter experts, conduct reference searches on potential job candidates and business partners, find jobs, knowledge or groups to make you more productive.

"I was applying for a job and when advised of an interview, I searched for the organization on LinkedIn. I found the HR manager's profile and was able to learn more about him and the company. In the two days between the initial interview and the subsequent telephone call asking me to attend a second interview, I checked my profile on LinkedIn and found that the HR manager had viewed my LinkedIn profile."

(Nicky Morris, executive assistant)

Group discussions can be interesting and informative but can also waste your time when you have e-mails constantly updating you on discussions. Make a rule to send all the e-mails that have LinkedIn in the subject line to a separate folder so that you can look at them when you have time. You can also change LinkedIn settings so that you don't receive e-mail notifications or only get them weekly.

Angela Garry states: 'LinkedIn has enabled me to become a regional chair for EUMA by meeting and developing relationships online. It has also enabled me to meet and work with some talented and inspiring people who are very influential in the PA and Training world.'

Other useful tools

'Yammer' is a free online internal network that lets you connect securely with your colleagues either privately or within groups. It reduces the need for internal meetings, increases communication, highlights areas of expertise and connects remote workers. You can share documents with colleagues, groups or your entire company. It also has free mobile apps so that you can connect anywhere, anytime. Perhaps you could suggest that your company use Yammer and offer to become a Yammer expert!

I would also like to recommend YouTube which is a very useful and valuable tool for watching videos and learning about most subjects you can think of, including how to use social media and how to set up profiles. It's also a valuable tool to promote yourself, your organization and your products/services. You can find two videos of me on You Tube which are linked to my website: **http://www.suefrance.com/videos-photos/**.

Carole Spiers states: 'Being a professional speaker, I have professional videos to upload and it is essential that I have a presence on YouTube. However, when my monitor broke, my PA found a YouTube video that showed us how to fix it in half an hour. So use YouTube for any of those questions that you or your boss might have. It is great for ideas, expanding your marketplace and for website optimization. Your boss should love it!'

Another great website for getting information is 'Quora', which is a cross between Twitter and Wikipedia (online encyclopaedia). It is a collection of questions and answers created, edited and organized by everyone who uses it and it is continually improving. You can sign up through Facebook or Twitter and follow subjects/people you are interested in. Eventually, when you see a link to a question page on Quora you will think 'Great – that's going to have all the information I want about that.'

Apps

Facebook and LinkedIn have developed powerful apps. An 'app' is an abbreviation for 'application'. It is a piece of software that can run on the internet, on your computer or on your phone or other electronic device and can help you in your everyday work. Apps are being created daily, so you have to explore and investigate what works well for you and your boss/ organization. For example, on my iPhone I use an app called Dragon Dictation – I can dictate into the phone, it translates it into text and I can either send an e-mail or text or store it as part of my to-do list.

You can download iPhone apps from Apple App Store and Android apps from the Android Market.

Facebook have a free 'Video Chat' app which is a videoconferencing engine. You'll be able to chat with your boss and see him or her at the same time. You can use the public tab viewing for more than one and you can have a one-to-one chat using the private tab.

An example of a LinkedIn app is 'Company Buzz'. This app lets you know what your customers are saying about your company. Every second, thousands of people are sending out messages about companies and industries on blogs, Twitter, and across the internet. Company Buzz taps into this information for you, to find the relevant trends and comments about your company. Another example is box.net which allows you to share documents and images.

You can get Twitter on your mobile phone through SMS/text messaging or with a third-party app. The app allows you to receive tweets from people/companies you follow, and also to post updates to Twitter from your phone.

Warning

You should read the fine print closely on all social media and in particular with the use of 'apps' connected to Twitter, LinkedIn and Facebook. For example, when we 'download/authorize' an app we are granting it 'permission'. Social sharing is posed as a positive part of some apps and they can operate in the background. Depending on how far each app takes auto-sharing, we might be posting status updates that we don't realize. To stay safe, lock down your privacy settings and read before you click.

What you can use social media for

"Social media = virtual brainstorming + global resource library. What innovative assistant doesn't want access to that!?"
(Kemetia M K Foley CPS/CAP, Executive Assistant – IAAP Chapter Leader – Washington, DC, United States)

There are many business reasons for being involved with social media and below are suggestions and examples:

- Update social media for your boss, whether it is writing blogs, completing the boss's profiles or writing Twitter updates and much more. Executive assistant Adam Fidler agrees and says that Twitter has become essential in promoting the work his company does. He is responsible for checking his boss's Twitter account daily and also for composing his boss's tweets.

- Share your knowledge and help other people (remember the law of reciprocation).

- Find new work/new job (and you may not even be looking for something but someone could find you). Having LinkedIn recommendations will help in a job search and the URL you can get also keeps you current and shows your potential employer that you are social media savvy.

- Networking – connecting with like-minded people and similar networking groups – for example, assistant groups such as EUMA, IAAP, AIOP, OPSA etc.

- Connecting with old friends/colleagues and alumni. Alumni are an extremely good source for developing new business and even obtaining a new job.

- Research on subjects, problems, ideas, training, advice and products.

- Marketing – Duda Jadrijevic, who is a 'virtual assistant', states that social media help to grow her business by raising her profile in a competitive market, raising the awareness of the existence of her services and enabling her to explain what she can do for others.

- Find recommended services, trainers and suppliers.

- Track what people are saying about you and your company. You can create free Google alerts so that whenever you or your company is mentioned, you will be sent an e-mail.

- Interact with your customer base and act as liaison officer to the public.

- Promote other content you've created, including webinars, blog posts or podcasts.

- Develop direct relationships with bloggers and journalists for potential PR.

- Generate sales leads for your business.

- Drive people to your or your company's website. Talk about interesting resources you've posted on a blog or website, e-books, newsletters, webinars that people can download for free. If they like your content, people may share your resources to their connections.

- Many journalists, reporters and bloggers make themselves available on Twitter, so why not introduce yourself and your company to the media – look for influential blogs in your industry and start following their authors on Twitter.

- Watch for editorial opportunities as it's a great place for media professionals to look for last-minute, additional resources for their stories.

- Twitter can be very useful when planning travel and accommodation for your boss, especially when the weather and acts of God affect travel, such as the snow crisis that grounded flights throughout the UK and the ash cloud that affected passengers' flights worldwide. Call centres struggled to cope with the call volumes and websites were slow to be updated, leaving thousands of passengers frustrated and unsure what was happening. Twitter was the one shining light as airlines, airports and travel companies with dedicated Twitter feeds worked tirelessly to keep passengers up to date with information. As Twitter works on mobile devices, savvy travellers who used Twitter were in the know sooner than those waiting on the phone or for the website updates – see how Twitter has been used for travel in the case study below.

"I currently work as a Marketing Executive at Gray Dawes and am responsible for updating the Twitter feed. We use Twitter to update our clients on airline or airport strikes, travel delays and anything else that may disrupt their business trip."

(Ben Williams)

You could have a 'trip'-specific Twitter account whereby you follow organizations specific to the trip your boss is undertaking and then the information they 'tweet' is likely to be relevant. Follow the travel management company, the airline they are flying with, the departure and arrival airports, the Foreign and Commonwealth Office and the hotel they are staying in. This way you can be sure that you are the first to hear about any issues that may arise and act accordingly to make the trip as seamless as possible.

Organize events using social media

Social media can enhance real-time events and open a whole new world for developing virtual events. There are clear benefits from incorporating social media before, during and after the event by allowing people to connect in powerful ways to help increase awareness, and they support traditional marketing.

You can create an event page where you can list the details of an event – date, time, location – everything you need to know to turn up at the right place, at the right time, on the right day and to reply whether they are attending or not.

Tools and software such as 'Eventbrite' can be used to register delegates. Twitter hashtags can be used to spread the word about the event and you can even use social media tools to help shape events and conduct simple polls afterwards, for example SurveyMonkey, PollDaddy and TwtPoll. You can have a person tweeting live throughout the event using an event-specific hashtag and you can reiterate key messages and continue to promote sponsors afterwards.

'Slideshare' can be used to upload presentations and even if your event is being held outside, with no traditional conference facilities, you can use 'QR Codes' to share the presentation without a projector and anyone with a smartphone can see it. You can give access to the presentations with links to videos and make your website the main place for post-event catch-up by using Ustream and YouTube.

By setting up an official Flickr page you can encourage participants to upload their own photos; you can quickly build a great unofficial photo record of the event, which you can use again in future promotions.

You can consider opening your real-time event to include virtual attendees or having a totally virtual event. You can have virtual exhibition halls where you can talk to people in real time using microphones and even see people using your cameras. You can attend virtual auditoriums to attend seminars and even have break-out rooms to work in smaller groups.

Opportunities, ideas and innovation are endless and there is so much to explore and learn around social media, and they are constantly evolving. It's about being aware and understanding what is happening in today's world. Take it upon yourself to research what is available, how best to use it and to continually learn and develop. You should be able to suggest to your boss and your company ways in which they could use social media to their advantage.

Jasmine Freeman, chief executive assistant to Joan Burge, Office Dynamics, states: 'Social media may not be a fit for everyone but most can think of ways to shape them to make them work for them – whether it be a marketing tool that brings in leads, relationship builder, brand awareness, or otherwise. We are responsible for knowing what we expect to get out of our social networks and then to create an action plan. If I want to get to know assistants in my industry or region and build relationships – I need to proactively devise a plan of action and then set that plan into motion to make it happen. The amazing thing about social media is that if you follow those steps and put in the time – it will work.'

Social media are an extremely important and low-cost tool that has a direct impact on our personal and business lives. It keeps you up to date on a daily basis with the current thinking and with expert opinion from all over the world. All companies and individuals not actively engaged in social media are missing a huge opportunity.

The power of social media is increasing and evolving by the day and companies are looking for social media savvy assistants – so make sure that you are a master of change and not a victim of change.

13 The future of the assistant

Bosses are looking for a super-efficient, effective and powerful partnership where you support each other and have fun working towards a common vision. It's the joining together of two people in a close partnership to combine complementary skills, knowledge and behaviours that creates the right chemistry to ensure success in working together towards joint objectives and goals in the most appropriate and efficient way.

"For our own success to be real, it must contribute to the success of others."
(Eleanor Roosevelt)

Communication

In a new role it takes time to find your feet. It doesn't happen overnight but you can help it along by being honest, earning trust and respect by being enthusiastic, well mannered, polite and with a 'can do/will do' proactive attitude, exceeding your own and your boss's expectations. All this will help you develop an effective working relationship with your boss. This starts at the interview, where you need to display excellent communication skills and body language, and thereafter develops by constant communication, using face-to-face meetings, the telephone, e-mail, voice messages and even text messages to keep each other informed and up to date.

It is vital to communicate constantly what is expected of each other and to set boundaries and rules; if either of you doesn't know the rules you won't succeed. Don't allow your boss to 'psychic manage' – you can't mind read! Instead, you need to listen actively; don't be afraid to ask questions, and repeat instructions back so as to make clear what you think the other person means, especially if you are unsure. This will ensure that you both know what is expected of you.

Smile a lot, use humour and have fun. This goes a long way to help build relationships and makes other people want to be around you, as well as making you feel good. People will feel that you are approachable and friendly. Choose to be happy when you wake up – life is too short for anything else.

Keeping up to date

A good assistant has to be proficient in all technical areas and computer packages, and to be keen to learn about new technology. Similarly, you should make sure that your boss is abreast of technical development, social media, new gadgets and electronic equipment. You also need to keep up to date and informed about the business world you work in. Read your business's industry magazines/articles, local business news and national papers like the *Financial Times*, as well as books, newsletters and secretarial magazines such as *Executive Secretary* magazine (purely training).

Learning is the essence of life and makes us what we are. Decide on areas (perhaps ones you have read about in this book) that you would like to explore/improve/work on. Transfer these into SMARTER goals using the pro forma goal-setting form, and take ownership and responsibility for your own learning and personal development. You can make use of the PDP (Appendix 2) to structure this.

In summary, the more skills you have as an assistant, the more employable you are. If you can demonstrate that you are 'social media savvy' on your CV, you have an extra string to your bow and are ready for the future.

Whenever there is change, embrace it. The only thing that is permanent is change.

Organizing for success

Be assertive and focus on solutions; be flexible and prepared to compromise. At the same time, take ownership and don't lay blame or make excuses.

Forward planning and organizational skills are key. You need to be prepared, so think in detail and think about things as if you were the person receiving your efforts and arrangements – put yourself in the other person's shoes. Pre-empt any possible problems and solve them with the minimum of fuss.

Don't let problems get out of hand and fester. The 'Problem-solving master' (Appendix 5) can help you be focused, systemic, objective and creative in finding the most effective solution, acting on it and evaluating it.

You have to use time efficiently if you are to meet all deadlines. The time management tools and techniques in this book include the 'Task prioritization matrix guide' (Figure 5.1), which you can use as your daily to-do list. Keeping time management under control will keep you stress free, healthy, organized and extremely efficient.

Yourself and others

Nourish yourself, and embrace continual development and self-development. Give and receive constructive feedback. Don't be defensive.

Be self-aware, recognizing your own strengths and weaknesses. It is useful to complete the 'Personal strengths assessment' form (Appendix 1), which helps you identify your weaknesses so that you can work on them and make them into strengths. Build on your self-confidence and get rid of any negative gremlins by using your positive coach. Use the power of the subconscious mind and use affirmations personal to you to constantly increase your belief in yourself!

You should always come to work well dressed and groomed. That gives you a feeling of power and of being in control. It also means that others will perceive you as smart, organized and professional. If you look the part you will feel the part.

Learn to influence difficult people effectively. If you have a conflict, use the 'Assertiveness, problem-solving and conflict management' strategy (Figure 4.1) to guide you through the process so as to achieve the most mutually beneficial win–win outcome. Remember that it's about having respect for yourself and each other.

Networking and career development

"Training and development are paramount if you are to enjoy a successful career as an assistant at the highest levels. The role will continue to evolve at a rapid pace as it has done over the past 10 years and will look completely different even in the next five years. It is essential that assistants are open to the variety of the role, learning and embracing new skills and change. I personally have found success by networking with other assistants internally and externally, sharing best practice and exchanging ideas on how to work more effectively. Having a commercial awareness plus an understanding of key processes and practices of a business will ensure success and longevity in your role."
(Victoria Darragh, 'Outstanding Contribution to the PA Profession'
– Mayfair PA Awards 2011)

One of the most useful things you can do is actively network and build relationships within and outside your organization. Join secretarial networking organizations like EUMA, Australian Institute of Office Professionals, International Association of Administrative Professionals (United States), Association for Office Professionals of South Africa and many more throughout the world. These organizations encourage you to share knowledge with like-minded individuals and offer opportunities to learn new skills and practise them in a safe environment. These include activities such as organizing events, being a committee member and chairing meetings. They can also give you the opportunity to travel and mix with different cultures.

Use social media for online networking, which can lead to face-to-face networking and vice versa. Remember to adhere to your company's social media policies and procedures and if you don't have any, think about writing them for your company.

Make your role into whatever it is you want it to be. Look for new challenges, increase your skill set and take on as much responsibility as you want. Make suggestions if you can see that things can be improved, whether directly or indirectly connected to your role. Think – how can you make a difference?

Be accountable for your actions and take responsibility for your decisions.

The future of the personal assistant/ executive assistant/secretary

The advance of technology and social media is changing the role of the assistant, and it is still as important as ever. There will always be a need for assistants, either in the more traditional role of diary management and PA-type duties or as office managers, project managers, event managers etc. Today's assistants have many more varied tasks to fulfil than they ever did; they need to keep on learning, developing and being multi-skilled. They often have university degrees and are able to speak more than one language. They usually have the most important problem-solving skills and are the first to know exactly what is going on in the company, whether because they work for the top people and have access to confidential information or because they 'keep their ears to the ground' and know what's going on in the organization as a whole – through the 'grapevine'.

In many cases, assistants are as skilled as the bosses they work for, and the relationship can become more like a partnership. Their thoughts, ideas and suggestions are valued by bosses. Assistants are the lynchpin of many businesses as they know the organizations and their bosses inside out.

The position of assistants is finally getting the recognition it deserves. They were originally called secretaries because they were the holders of secrets; they still fulfil that role but also do much more. They are the boss's right hand and are highly qualified, whether in examinations passed or experience gained or both. The titles they are given differ but, whatever title you have, it's the job that you do and the role that you play and how well you do it that really matter.

> *"A modern assistant will need to be able to adapt to this change in role and move with it. Very interesting and exciting times lie ahead for those assistants who are up to this."*
>
> (Derek Knowles)

> *"The role of the assistant will continue to be an ever-changing one, adapting to the boss, environment, challenges and technology."*
>
> (Carol Gourlay)

The future of the assistant is in your own hands – if you keep aware of new trends in technology and social media, continually learn, make and achieve goals, embrace and adapt to change, you can be whoever you want to be and do whatever you want to do. One thing is for sure, it's up to you to take responsibility for your own destiny.

Apply your heart, soul and mind to develop, believe in and value yourself and have the confidence to achieve your goals while remembering to have fun and laughter on life's exciting journey.

Also remember to 'connect' with me on LinkedIn, 'follow' me on Twitter and be my 'friend' on Facebook!

Best wishes for your exciting future.

Sue France, FCIPD, INLPTA
International Trainer and Coach for Admin Professionals (www.suefrance.com), Certified TetraMap® Facilitator, Qualified Chartered Institute of Personnel and Development – Learning and Development Practitioner, Certified Neuro-Linguistic Programming Practitioner, Associate Trainer for Reed Learning UK, National UK Chairman for European Management Assistants (www.euma.org), Editorial Board Member for *Executive Secretary* Magazine (Training Magazine) (www.executivesecreatary.com).

APPENDIX 1
Personal strengths assessment form

You can access these forms online. Be honest. Respond with your first impression. Do NOT spend a lot of time thinking about each statement.

1	2	3	4	5	6	7	8	9
Not at all characteristic	Somewhat characteristic	Characteristic about ½ the time		Characteristic				Very characteristic

Respond with your first impression. Do **NOT** spend a lot of time thinking about each statement.

1	2	3	4	5	6	7	8	9	**1.**	I approach others with confidence
1	2	3	4	5	6	7	8	9	**2.**	I act spontaneously
1	2	3	4	5	6	7	8	9	**3.**	I solve problems
1	2	3	4	5	6	7	8	9	**4.**	I make daily plans for learning and growing
1	2	3	4	5	6	7	8	9	**5.**	I express my feelings and opinions clearly
1	2	3	4	5	6	7	8	9	**6.**	I am myself in a wide range of situations
1	2	3	4	5	6	7	8	9	**7.**	I am aware of my values and goals
1	2	3	4	5	6	7	8	9	**8.**	I act with confidence in many situations
1	2	3	4	5	6	7	8	9	**9.**	I listen, even under stress

1	2	3	4	5	6	7	8	9	**10.**	I accept myself and my feelings
1	2	3	4	5	6	7	8	9	**11.**	I organize my time so I can achieve my goals
1	2	3	4	5	6	7	8	9	**12.**	I handle conflicts with others
1	2	3	4	5	6	7	8	9	**13.**	I work closely with others and share tasks
1	2	3	4	5	6	7	8	9	**14.**	I trust myself in a wide range of situations
1	2	3	4	5	6	7	8	9	**15.**	I think about options in the decisions I am facing
1	2	3	4	5	6	7	8	9	**16.**	I accept the challenge of making decisions and have the skills to make decisions
1	2	3	4	5	6	7	8	9	**17.**	I express concern for others
1	2	3	4	5	6	7	8	9	**18.**	I am open both to myself and to others
1	2	3	4	5	6	7	8	9	**19.**	I visualize and think through problems
1	2	3	4	5	6	7	8	9	**20.**	I carry a plan of action through to completion, despite setbacks
1	2	3	4	5	6	7	8	9	**21.**	I am friendly to others
1	2	3	4	5	6	7	8	9	**22.**	I am creative, curious and interested
1	2	3	4	5	6	7	8	9	**23.**	I organize my learning in a systematic manner
1	2	3	4	5	6	7	8	9	**24.**	I accept responsibility for myself and my actions
1	2	3	4	5	6	7	8	9	**25.**	I help those around me
1	2	3	4	5	6	7	8	9	**26.**	I treat myself with respect
1	2	3	4	5	6	7	8	9	**27.**	I influence others
1	2	3	4	5	6	7	8	9	**28.**	I act with self-control and personal power

Scoring grid

Transfer your scores to the appropriate section below:

1. People interaction			2. Strengths that help you add value		
1.		Approaching people	2.		Spontaneity
5.		Express feelings and opinions	6.		Authenticity
9.		Listening	10.		Self-acceptance
13.		Sharing	14.		Trusting self
17.		Expressing caring	18.		Openness
21.		Personal	22.		Creative
25.		Love and caring	26.		Self-respect
Total =			**Total =**		

3. Critical thinking skills			4. Enhancing your confidence		
3.		Problem solving	4.		Planning
7.		Value/goal awareness	8.		Self-confidence
11.		Time management	12.		Handle conflicts
15.		Decision making	16.		Decisions
19.		Thinking skills	20.		Self-discipline
23.		Learning skills	24.		Responsibility
27.		Influencing skills	28.		Self-control
Total			**Total =**		

Total the scores in each of the four sections. Transfer the totals to the 'Self-esteem profile' by placing an X in its appropriate place. For example, if you received a total of 24 in 'People interaction' you would place your mark like this:

	10	20	30	40	50
1. People interaction		X			

	10	20	30	40	50
1. People interaction					
2. Strengths that help you add value					
3. Critical thinking skills					
4. Enhancing your confidence					

From this self-analysis, select several areas you wish to strengthen, list these areas on your personal development plan and create goals. Celebrate your strengths and strive to improve them to become the expert. Find out what your boss's weaknesses are and make them your strengths so that you can complement them.

APPENDIX 2
Personal development plan (PDP)

Name:

Purpose of PDP

To help you understand yourself and commit to and focus on your personal development/learning and training requirements. It will help you to assess gaps in your skills and experience as well as to focus on learning outcomes, to identify your strengths and to boost your self-confidence. You can use this PDP in your appraisal meetings and to help you in career management.

Table of contents

Section 1: Strengths and areas for development

You could complete and attach the 'Personal strengths assessment form' (Appendix 1), which identifies your strengths and outlines any areas that you need to develop. Alternatively, you can think about and list below your strengths and areas that you know you need to develop. Include any training/ knowledge and skills acquired over the last 12 months.

Note: You can read your list of strengths to boost your self-confidence.

Your strengths

For example: communication, negotiation, problem solving, decision making, time management, assertiveness, building relationships, leadership, questioning skills, listening skills, self-awareness and confidence, influencing skills, creative skills. Remember that some strengths, when over the top, can be perceived as weaknesses. For example, an overly confident person could be perceived as being unapproachable.

Areas you need to work on

For example: communication, negotiation, problem solving, decision making, time management, assertiveness, building relationships, leadership, questioning skills, listening skills, self-awareness and confidence, influencing skills, creative skills.

Section 2: Opportunities and threats

Opportunities

Write here any opportunities that you come across or think of that may aid you in your quest for continual development and help you reach your goals.

Threats

Write here any threats that may hinder your development or achievement of your goals. Think and write creatively about how you can turn these into opportunities or eliminate them.

Section 3: Reflecting back

- Complete this section to reflect on your learning.
- Understand what you need to do differently.
- It will also help you realize the value you add to your organization.

Q1   What do you consider were the three most important things (planned or unplanned) that you learnt last year? Please also briefly describe how they were learnt.

1

2

3

Q2 Please write down what you will do differently as a result of your learning outcomes.

Q3 What have been the tangible outcomes of your professional development over the last 12 months?

Q4 Who else has gained from your professional development and how?

Q5 Please summarize the value you've added to your organization/clients/customers over the last 12 months through your professional development.

Section 4: Your action plan

- Complete this section to plan your way forward.
- Commit to goal setting and achieving.

Q1 When and how do you identify your learning and professional development needs?

Q2 What are the three main areas or topics you wish to develop in the next 12 months and how will you achieve these? What training and development do you need? What experience do you need? How will you get the training and experience? This might be, for example, through reading, surfing the internet, on-the-job training, voluntary work, workshops, training courses, teaching others, online courses, mentors or coaches, joining a network for assistants.

1.

2.

3.

Q3   What are the key differences that you plan to make to your role/ organization/clients/customers in the next 12 months?

Section 5: Values and any other thoughts

Write your values here, and any other thoughts that you feel could help you with your PDP.

Section 6: Goal setting

You can attach your completed goal-setting pro forma (Appendix 4), which can be downloaded online and contains all the information you need to help set your goals, or you can briefly write your 'SMARTER' goals here.

Remember: goals should be Specific, Measurable, Achievable, Realistic, Timed, Evaluated and Revised.

You can share your goals with your boss. You should align some of your goals with your boss's and your organization's. For life goals, think about how it will be when you are sitting in your rocking chair at 90 years old: what would you wish you had done, seen, learnt?

Commitment

Please sign below. This will make your subconscious mind commit to this PDP.

You might like to write here a personal mission statement/personal motto/quote/affirmation.

Signature: ....

Date: ....

APPENDIX 3
Preferred communication style

I ndicate your preferred answer or answers by sharing a total of five points between A, B and C for each of the 20 questions.

You can allocate all five points to just one answer. For example:

A	B	C
5	0	0

Or you may want to share the five points between two or all three answers, eg:

A	B	C
2	2	1

	A	B	C
1 A job description covering the duties of a PA/EA/secretary should: a) Tell me what I have to do b) Show me the right way to do things c) Make me feel that I know what to do			
2 It is important to have a good relationship with all the people you work with because: a) A business works more smoothly that way b) It reflects the promise of good service c) Harmonious relationships mean happy colleagues/customers/clients			

3 In reality, you could probably find at least 10 things wrong with the business you work for. Then again: a) You could probably picture five things that are right b) You could probably describe five things that are right c) You could probably feel five things that are right	A	B	C
4 When shopping generally I tend to: a) Try on, handle it, feel it's right for me b) Discuss with shop staff and ask for opinions of others c) Look and decide	A	B	C
5 When understanding what my boss/customers want, I like to: a) Ask lots of questions about their needs and wants b) Get a good feel of what they want c) Get a full picture of their requirements	A	B	C
6 When operating new equipment for the first time I prefer to: a) Listen to or ask for an explanation b) Read the instructions c) Have a go and learn by 'trial and error'	A	B	C
7 When teaching someone to do something I prefer to: a) Demonstrate and let them have a go b) Explain verbally c) Write the instructions down	A	B	C
8 When learning a new skill I prefer to: a) watch what the teacher is doing b) talk through with the teacher exactly what I am supposed to do c) give it a try and work it out as I go along by doing it	A	B	C
9 I first notice how people: a) Look and dress b) Stand and move c) Sound and speak	A	B	C

10 When choosing from a menu:	A	B	C
a) I imagine what the food will taste like b) I imagine what the food will look like c) I talk through the options in my head			
11 I remember things best by:	A	B	C
a) Writing notes or keeping printed details b) Saying them aloud or repeating words and key points in my head c) Doing and practising the activity, or imagining it being done			
12 When concentrating:	A	B	C
a) I move around a lot, fiddle with pens and pencils and touch unrelated things b) I focus on the words or pictures in front of me c) I discuss the problem and possible solutions in my head			
13 If I am angry:	A	B	C
a) I stomp about, slam doors and throw things b) I shout lots and tell people how I feel c) I keep replaying in my mind what it is that has upset me			
14 Most PAs/EAs/secretaries would be far more interested in doing something if they:	A	B	C
a) Could see the benefit to them personally b) Felt that they would get a benefit c) Were told of the personal benefits			
15 When anxious:	A	B	C
a) I talk over in my head what worries me most b) I visualize the worst-case scenarios c) I can't sit still, fiddle and move around constantly			
16 I find it easier to remember:	A	B	C
a) Faces b) Names c) Things I have done			

17 When it comes to finding out about something:	A	B	C
a) I would understand much better if I could see it b) I want to try it before I can fully understand it c) I would prefer to have someone explain it to me			
18 When it comes to finding my way somewhere:	A	B	C
a) It's no problem if I have a map b) I need someone to tell me the way and I ask people c) I just know if I have got it right and I 'follow my nose'			
19 When I have a problem to solve:	A	B	C
a) I often talk it over with myself b) I can visualize the answer c) I think it through until I can feel the right answer			
20 Contented bosses/customers/clients are:	A	B	C
a) What we all want to see at the end of the day b) What everybody wants to hear about c) The way to a smooth future			

Your ranking of senses?

To find out your own preferred method of processing the world, simply fill in the scores that you allocated to each of the three alternative answers to the 20 questions, then add up the scores to identify your own preference.

Visual		Auditory		Kinaesthetic	
1 B		A		C	
2 B		C		A	
3 A		B		C	
4 C		B		A	

Visual		Auditory		Kinaesthetic	
5 C		A		B	
6 B		A		C	
7 C		B		A	
8 A		B		C	
9 A		C		B	
10 B		C		A	
11 A		B		C	
12 B		C		A	
13 C		B		A	
14 A		C		B	
15 B		A		C	
16 A		B		C	
17 A		C		B	
18 A		B		C	
19 B		A		C	
20 A		B		C	
Totals					

It is most likely that you have scored many of the points in the same column. The largest of your three totals indicates the sense that you prefer to use to communicate and to input information into your brain.

Preferred style

Your learning style also reflects the type of person you are, how you perceive things and how you relate to the world and to other people.

Visual Seeing and reading Visual learning style involves the use of seen or observed things, including pictures, diagrams, demonstrations, displays, handouts, films, flip charts etc	
Auditory Listening and speaking Auditory learning style involves the transfer of information through listening: to the spoken word, of self or others, of sounds and noises	
Kinaesthetic Touching and doing Kinaesthetic learning involves physical experience – touching, feeling, holding, doing, practical hands-on experiences	

APPENDIX 4
Pro forma for goal setting

Goal setting is an important method of:

- deciding what is important for you to achieve in your working life;
- separating what is important for you from what is irrelevant;
- motivating yourself to achievement;
- building your self-confidence through measured achievement of goals.

Guidelines for setting goals

- Write them down in the present tense and positively.
- Define them precisely.
- Prioritize multiple goals.
- Split larger goals into smaller achievable chunks.
- Keep them manageable: not too hard, but not too easy.
- Write down why you want to achieve your goals. What will achieving each goal do for you emotionally, financially and spiritually?
- Think about who can support you.
- You can share your goals with your boss. You should align some of your goals with your boss's and your organization's.
- Visualize your goals. To trigger your imagination and creativity, write out a clear description of your ideal end result; be clear about the goal but flexible about the process. Visualize achieving it over and over.
- Imagine yourself 90 years old and sitting in your rocking chair. Think about what you would wish you had done, seen, learnt. What would you have regretted not doing?

When setting goals the following should be taken into consideration so as to set 'SMARTER' goals.

Specific/stretching

The goal should be specific, as this makes it easier to recognize and achieve. For example:

> *Check the stationery cupboard every day just before going back to my desk after lunch; make sure it's tidy and order anything that we are running short of in good time.*

Just writing 'ensure stationery supplies are available' is not sufficient.

'S' can also stand for a 'stretched' goal to 'stretch' your capabilities. Thus you can add to this example a decision to look at the stationery suppliers and check you are getting value for money, and possibly to change suppliers or negotiate to buy different brands. When we stretch ourselves we rise to the challenge and increase our motivation, which in turn gives us confidence in our abilities when we succeed. Success breeds success and we feel exhilarated when we achieve more than we realized we could.

Measurable/meaningful/motivating

A goal has to be measured to know that you have achieved it. What are you measuring your goal against? How will you know when you have reached it? It has to be meaningful and motivating in order to satisfy the need to know why it should be done. What motivation do you need?

In the example above, it would be that everyone finds the stationery area tidy at all times and that there are always plenty of supplies of whatever is needed at any time. Also, there would be no need to worry about the state of the area if anyone coming in for a meeting has to walk past it to get to the boardroom.

Achievable/acceptable/agreed/accountable

If you are to take responsibility for pursuit of a goal, the goal has to be acceptable to you and must be achievable. What do you need in order to achieve it? You may need to have it agreed by your boss, depending on what it affects and whether there is a budget involved. You should take responsibility and be held accountable for setting and reaching the goal by the set deadline, or at least be involved in setting the target. You may need to change or work around your other commitments or modify other goals to achieve it.

Break your goal down into smaller steps if it is too big. Sometimes confidence is knocked because goals are too big or there are too many of them. You need to believe that they are achievable. Decide how many goals it is realistic for you to be working on at any one time.

Realistic/relevant/results-oriented/responsible

Even if you do accept responsibility for something specific and measurable, it won't be useful to anyone if, for example, the goal is to 'complete a 30-page report in the next five minutes'. It has to be realistic and relevant to your role and to your aims and objectives. The aim is to achieve results. In the goal we have set above, this would mean that the stationery cupboard will always have sufficient supplies to meet demand and do so in the most cost-effective way.

Time frame

You need to specify the time frame for a goal, such as when you will check the area and how often: would it (realistically) be every day or every other day? Would it be first thing in the morning, after lunch or at the end of the day?

For some goals you will need a specific time and date. Do not just put a rough date; you must have an actual project deadline such as 5.30 pm on Tuesday 29 May 2012.

Set a realistic timescale, establishing short-term targets with stated dates by which they are to be accomplished. Perhaps set a three-year goal and work backwards until you get to daily tasks that can be checked upon frequently. This will give you a sense both of urgency and of achievement, as well as a clear idea of how you will get to the end result.

Evaluate/extend/enthusiastic

All goals should be monitored and evaluated on an ongoing basis, but you should also set yourself a specific time to re-evaluate your objectives and goals. Be flexible because life is always changing – if you are too rigid about your goals you can end up missing out on opportunities.

Revise/reward/record

After evaluating the goal you may find that you need to revise and change it (if it is appropriate to move the goalposts), as things around us change all the time and the only thing that is permanent is change.

Once the goal has been achieved, meeting all criteria and within the time frame, you should be rewarded, whether by just a 'pat on the back', a piece of chocolate that you might not otherwise allow yourself, lunch out in a nice restaurant, treating yourself to a new outfit for work or whatever it is that you prefer as a reward.

Tips on setting goals

- List your tasks.
- Which of the tasks do you think could be improved upon?
- How could you make this improvement happen?

Using the guidelines, follow the action plan below for each goal:

What is your 'SMARTER' goal?

What is the purpose of the goal and what are the benefits of achieving it?

What will achieving your goal do for you emotionally, financially and spiritually?

What skills, competencies, abilities, beliefs, knowledge etc do you need to achieve the goal?

What immediate action can you take?

What steps are necessary to achieve this goal and what is the time frame?

Who will hold you accountable for this goal (it could be yourself)?

Skill competencies

List some of the skill competencies that you wish to improve upon at the start of your goal setting.

List some of the skill competencies that you have improved upon at completion of the goal.

Signed at start of goal process by: _____

Date goal completed: _____

APPENDIX 5
Problem-solving master

The following problem-solving technique can help you be objective and systematic when dealing with difficult people and any kind of problem you want to solve:

Describe the perceived problem as briefly as possible:

Disengage your emotions from the problem and give objective facts relevant to the problem, giving specific examples if possible:

List all possible reasons and causes of the problem you can think of:

Objective: describe positively and concisely what you want the end outcome to be:

Be creative and 'mind storm' as many solutions as possible below and include all points of view (some you may not agree with or like but you still have to consider them):

Write down all risks and benefits associated with each solution:

Possible solutions	Risks	Benefits

Choose the most appropriate solution taking into consideration the risks and benefits and write it below:

Action plan: Identify who does what by when, where and how it is to be done and action it!

Who	What	When	Where	How

Evaluate how it went, learn from mistakes and revise action plan if necessary.

APPENDIX 6
Positive adjectives/action verbs

Here is a list of positive adjectives that you can use in your profile, personal branding and/or company branding as well as your CV to describe you/your company.

> The words you choose about yourself are very useful for you to read to help you boost your self-esteem and confidence about yourself.

Affable
Agreeable
Alert
Ambitious
Approachable
Articulate
Artistic
Attentive
Brave
Bright
Calm
Capable
Careful
Cautious
Charming
Cheerful
Clever
Competent
Confident
Confidant
Considerate

Contented
Cooperative
Courteous
Courageous
Creative
Credible
Decisive
Delightful
Dependable
Detailed
Determined
Diligent
Direct
Discreet
Dynamic
Eager
Earnest
Easy-going
Efficient
Elated
Eminent

Enchanting

Encouraging

Energetic

Engaging

Entertaining

Enthusiastic

Excellent

Excited

Expert (state what in)

Extrovert

Fair

Faithful

Fearless

Flexible

Forgiving

Friendly

Funny

Generous

Gentle

Good

Good-natured

Guru

Happy

Hard-working

Harmonious

Helpful

Hilarious

Honourable

Honest

Hospitable

Honourable

Image-conscious

Imaginative

Impartial

Industrious

Instinctive

Intelligent

Interesting

Introverted (this is a good trait in some circumstances)

Jolly

Joyous

Kind

Kind-hearted

Knowledgeable

Level-headed

Likeable

Literate

Lively

Logical

Loyal

Mature personality

Modern

Modest (but not too modest that you cannot write this list!)

Obedient

Outgoing

Open-minded

Optimistic

Organized

Passionate

Patient

Placid

Plausible

Pleasant

Polite

Positive

Practical

Productive

Proper

Protective

Proud

Punctual

Quiet

Receptive

Reflective

Relaxed

Reliable

Reserved

Resourceful

Respectful
Responsible
Self-assured
Sensible
Sensitive
Serious
Shrewd
Sincere
Skilled
Smart
Smiling
Sophisticated
Splendid
Spontaneous
Steadfast
Stimulating
Street-smart
Strong
Successful
Succinct
Tactful

Talented
Thoughtful
Thrifty
Tolerant
Tough
Trusting
Trustworthy
Unbiased
Unusual
Upbeat
Vigorous
Virtues
Vivacious
Warm-hearted
Well mannered
Well presented
Willing
Wise
Witty
Wonderful

The following are action verbs that you can include in your profile/CV regarding your achievements:

Accelerated
Accomplished
Accounted for
Accumulated
Achieved
Acquired
Acted
Activated
Active in
Adapted
Addressed
Adjusted
Administered
Advanced

Advertised
Advised
Advocated
Affected
Aided
Alerted
Allocated
Altered
Amplified
Analyzed
Answered
Anticipated
Applied
Appointed

Appraised

Approved

Arbitrated

Arranged

Articulated

Ascertained

Aspired

Assembled

Assessed

Assigned

Assisted

Assumed responsibility

Assured

Attained

Attracted

Authored

Automated

Awarded

Balanced

Billed

Boosted

Bought

Briefed

Broadened

Budgeted

Built

Calculated

Campaigned

Captured

Carried out

Caused

Centralized

Chaired

Championed

Changed

Charted

Checked

Clarified

Classified

Closed

Coached

Co-directed

Collaborated

Collected

Co-managed

Combined

Commanded

Commended

Commented

Communicated

Compared

Compiled

Completed

Composed

Computed

Conceived

Conceptualized

Condensed

Conducted

Conferred

Conserved

Considered

Consolidated

Constructed

Consulted

Contacted

Contained

Contracted

Contributed

Controlled

Converted

Coordinated

Corrected

Correlated

Corresponded

Counselled

Counted

Created

Critiqued
Crowned
Cultivated
Cured
Customized
Cut
Dealt with
Decreased
Defined
Delegated
Delivered
Demonstrated
Described
Designated
Designed
Detected
Determined
Developed
Devised
Diagnosed
Directed
Discovered
Dispatched
Dispensed
Displayed
Dissected
Distinguished
Distributed
Documented
Doubled
Drafted
Drove
Earned
Economized
Edited
Educated
Effected
Eliminated
Emphasized

Employed
Empowered
Enabled
Enacted
Encouraged
Ended
Endorsed
Energized
Enforced
Engaged
Engineered
Enhanced
Enlarged
Enlisted
Ensured
Entertained
Established
Estimated
Evaluated
Examined
Exceeded
Executed
Expanded
Expedited
Experienced
Experimented
Explained
Explored
Expressed
Extended
Extracted
Facilitated
Familiarized
Filled
Finalized
Fine-tuned
Fixed
Focused
Forecasted

Formed

Formulated

Fostered

Found

Founded

Fulfilled

Functioned as

Furnished

Gained

Gathered

Generated

Graded

Graduated

Granted

Grew

Guided

Halved

Handled

Harmonized

Harnessed

Headed

Helped

Hired

Identified

Illustrated

Imagined

Implemented

Impressed

Improved

Improvised

Incorporated

Increased

Indexed

Indoctrinated

Influenced

Informed

Initiated

Innovated

Inspected

Inspired

Installed

Instigated

Instituted

Instructed

Insured

Integrated

Interpreted

Interviewed

Introduced

Invented

Invested

Investigated

Involved

Issued

Joined

Judged

Justified

Launched

Lead

Learned

Leased

Lectured

Led

Liaised

Licensed

Listed

Located

Logged

Made

Magnified

Maintained

Managed

Marketed

Mastered

Matched

Maximized

Measured

Mediated

Merged

Met

Minimized

Mobilized

Moderated

Modernized

Modified

Monitored

Motivated

Moved

Named

Navigated

Negated

Negotiated

Observed

Obtained

Opened

Operated

Optimized

Orchestrated

Ordered

Organized

Originated

Outlined

Overhauled

Oversaw

Participated

Perceived

Performed

Persuaded

Photographed

Piloted

Pinpointed

Pioneered

Placed

Planned

Predicted

Prepared

Presented

Presided

Prevented

Printed

Prioritized

Processed

Procured

Produced

Programmed

Prohibited

Projected

Promoted

Proofread

Proposed

Protected

Proved

Provided

Publicized

Published

Purchased

Pursued

Qualified

Queried

Questioned

Raised

Ran

Ranked

Rated

Reached

Realigned

Realized

Reasoned

Received

Recognized

Recommended

Reconciled

Recorded

Recruited

Redesigned

Reduced

Referred

Registered

Regulated

Rehabilitated

Reinforced

Related

Remodelled

Rendered

Reorganized

Repaired

Replaced

Replied

Reported

Represented

Reputed

Researched

Resolved

Responded

Restored

Restructured

Retrieved

Revamped

Reversed

Reviewed

Revised

Revitalized

Saved

Scheduled

Screened

Searched

Secured

Selected

Separated

Served

Serviced

Set up

Shaped

Shared

Showed

Simplified

Simulated

Sketched

Slashed

Sold

Solidified

Solved

Sorted

Sought

Spearheaded

Specialized

Specified

Spoke

Sponsored

Staffed

Standardized

Started

Steered

Stimulated

Stored

Streamlined

Strengthened

Stressed

Stretched

Structured

Studied

Submitted

Substituted

Succeeded

Suggested

Summarized

Superseded

Supervised

Supplemented

Supplied

Supported

Surpassed

Surveyed

Synchronized

Synergized

Systemized

Tabulated

Tackled

Targeted

Taught

Terminated

Tested

Tightened

Took over

Totalled

Traced

Tracked

Traded

Trained

Transcribed

Transferred

Transformed

Translated

Transmitted

Transported

Travelled

Treated

Triggered

Trimmed

Tripled

Triumphed

Troubleshot

Turned

Tutored

Typed

Umpired

Uncovered

Understood

Understudied

Undertook

Underwent

Unearthed

Unified

United

Unravelled

Updated

Upgraded

Urged

Used

Utilized

Validated

Valued

Verbalized

Verified

Visited

Vitalized

Volunteered

Widened

Won

Worked

Wrote

INDEX

NB: page numbers in *italic* indicate figures or tables